COUNTRY INNS
of
MARYLAND, VIRGINIA & WEST VIRGINIA

By Lewis Perdue

WASHINGTONIAN BOOKS

ABOUT THE AUTHOR

Lewis Perdue has written for *The Nation, The Washington Post, Travel* magazine, *Backpacking Journal, Country Gentleman, Popular Mechanics, Trailer Life,* Woodall's *Trailer and RV Travel,* and *The Washingtonian* magazine. He has coauthored a novel, *The Trinity Implosion,* with Robin Moore and writes a nationally syndicated weekly outdoor column.

Book Design: Ed Schneider
Cover Design: Phyllis Cox
Illustrations by John Heinly
Cover Engraving: Bettmann Archive

Published by Washingtonian Books
1828 L Street, N.W.
Washington, D.C. 20036

DEDICATION

To Shan, my wife and partner, who has been with me on
every single trip for the months of exhausting travel over back
roads and country lanes. And to my mother whose good cooking taught me to love eating.

Ta voglio tanto bene
tua figlia

♡
Candie L

El Paso Tex. 1977.

with Becky Lozano, R.J. & Family.

CONTENTS

RULES OF THE TAVERNS

Travelers will be welcomed as guests of the house

The owner will be your host

Patrons must leave city habits at home

Stories about the resident ghost and other famous guests will
be told upon request

Overnight lodgings will be provided, space permitting

Menu fare will change with the season to insure use of
fresh ingredients

Large helpings must be served to all diners

Breads and muffins will be hot from the oven

A draught of ale may be taken before dinner

Guests should warm themselves by the fire

A historic and personal atmosphere must be preserved

INTRODUCTION

Label this the hardest part of the book to write. I think it is easier to answer the question "what is the meaning of life" than the question "what is an inn?"

Inns have traditionally been thought to provide lodging, and historically this is accurate. Serving either as a stagecoach stop or merely as a way station for weary travelers, they provided facilities for the out-of-town visitor to take a bath, have a hot meal and a place to sleep during a time when getting there was *not* half the fun of traveling.

Inns also served a more local purpose. They functioned as meeting halls for businessmen and politicians, hosted social events, and were centers of underground activity during the American Revolution and, to a lesser extent, the Civil War. For these purposes the inn did not need to provide overnight accommodations, except possibly in the case of the fine gentleman who imbibed a bit too much to allow him to ride his horse back to his country home.

Because of this second more local function (which was the largest part of the innkeeper's business) I have decided to include in this book many inns that do not take overnight guests. And in a couple of cases, inns that take overnight guests but do not serve meals.

But what is it that differentiates an inn from an ordinary restaurant or hotel? There are a few factors that are paramount—friendliness, a feeling of being welcome more as a guest than as another patron. A place you go to for comfort and charm, or for authentic historical trappings. The following is a list of the most important factors:

Personalness. Okay, so you may not find this word in your Funk and Wagnalls, but you'll find its definition at inns. It's when the owners are the managers, maître d's, chief cooks, and bottle washers. They take a personal interest in their guests, have dinner with them, drop by their table for a few minutes, or take time in the evening to converse in the living room. Often they are husband-wife teams.

Smallness. To give a high degree of personal attention, an inn can't get too big. Probably fifteen rooms is optimum and forty is stretching things a bit thin.

Country location. Most of the inns in this book are really in the middle of nowhere. Some of them are in small rural towns, and only a handful are near large metropolitan areas. All retain a country atmosphere.

History. With only a couple of exceptions, the inns in this book have a history. Some are more historic than others—some have been associated with famous persons or events, and others are merely located in restored old buildings.

Little touches. Not all the food at inns rates rave reviews, but you can always expect a lot of attention given to detail. The use of antiques and reproductions in the décor, careful restorations of interiors, hot bread and desserts freshly baked in the inn's kitchen, fresh vegetables, napkin rings, butter knives, complimentary snacks in the room or taken with the innkeeper, lemon sherbet to cleanse the palate between courses, tea balls instead of bags, lime for hot tea, room accessories that show some thought was given to their selection, freshly ground pepper, and real butter.

Some other things my wife, Shan (who accompanied me on all trips), and I looked for in selecting the inns were: places that have ghost stories associated with them; remote or scenic locations; ethnicity of any sort, since Shan and I delight in learning about other cultures.

It's a good thing we didn't take an inn's name into account when we determined what places could be labeled inns. Two of the best we went to had very unlikely and disappointing names—Jim Bollinger's Oak Supper Club in Pipestem, West Virginia, and Maude's in Owing's Mills, Maryland. Now, the moniker "Supper Club" evokes images in my mind of cinder-block buildings with fluorescent lights. Something like "Maude's" reminds me of a grimy truck stop. Fortunately, both of these establishments rise far above the level of their names and soar to great heights of cooking and friendliness.

There are several terms that we've used interchangeably: inn, tavern, and ordinary. The differences are regional; generally, inn was the word used in New England, tavern was heard most frequently in the Middle Atlantic area and upper South, and ordinary was preferred in the deep South. I have used them all, sometimes in the description of the same inn.

In writing this book, we visited 108 establishments, some of which we did not consider inns and will not mention. If we have truly missed an inn, we want very much to hear from you so that it has a chance to be included in future editions.

Which brings us to the point of telling how we
tracked down all of these inns. We depended largely on
personal recommendations; we asked friends and just
about everyone we met on our travels—policemen, service
station attendants, owners of other inns, motel managers
—if they knew of any inns. As we drove through the
countryside, we often just stumbled over new ones. These
unexpected finds were pleasurable indeed. Much of our
beginning information was furnished by the tourism de-
partments of West Virginia and Virginia.

People have continuously asked me how we con-
ducted inspections of the inns. Unlike the leading inn
guide books on the market, we did not announce our
arrival or intentions and we did not ask for, expect, or
receive free meals or lodgings. Our conversations with
innkeepers took place only after we had paid for what
we had received, and after it was too late for the innkeepers to change anything.

In looking through the reviews of the food ordered
by us, you will undoubtedly notice the frequency of fish
and seafood dishes. One reason for this is that many
establishments offered these as specialties of the house,
and wherever possible we ate the house specialties. A second reason is that seafood goes bad fast and must be
fresh to be good, and is therefore a good test of the care
taken in buying and preparing food.

All of the inns except the ones in the "not recommended" section are inns that I personally would return
to, although I would favor some over others when given
a choice. I sincerely hope that the information contained
in this book will not only be of service to you, but will
help you enjoy an entirely new dimension in traveling
and vacationing.

Lewis Perdue
1977

AUTHOR'S CHOICE

BEST FOOD
Jim Bollinger's Oak Supper Club,
  Pipestem, West Virginia
Foxhead Inn, Manakin-Sabot, Virginia
Channel Bass Inn, Chincoteague, Virginia
Maude's, Owing's Mills, Maryland
L'Auberge Chez François, Great Falls, Virginia

BEST LODGING
Alexander-Withrow House, Lexington, Virginia

BEST COMBINATION OF FOOD AND LODGING
Maryland Inn, Annapolis, Maryland

MOST HISTORIC
Maryland Inn, Annapolis, Maryland
Red Fox Inn, Middleburg, Virginia

FRIENDLIEST
Jim Bollinger's Oak Supper Club,
  Pipestem, West Virginia
Strawberry Inn, New Market, Maryland

BEST BARGAIN
Laurel Brigade Inn, Leesburg, Virginia

MOST UNIQUE
Gristmill Square, Warm Springs, Virginia

MOST ROMANTIC
Milton Inn, Sparks, Maryland

BEST PLACE TO SPEND A TWO-WEEK VACATION
Mountain Creek Lodge, Pipestem, West Virginia

MOST HOMEY
Sky Chalet, Mount Jackson, Virginia

MOST RELAXING
Graves Mountain Lodge, Syria, Virginia

NOTES ON THE RATINGS AND SUMMARIES

In describing dress, informal means that men should wear coats and women should dress accordingly. Nice casual means sport shirts and slacks for men and sportswear for women. Nice casual to informal means that men don't need to wear a coat but might feel more comfortable wearing one.

Unless otherwise mentioned, assume that rooms have private baths but do not have televisions. When going to an inn where overnight accommodations are on a shared bath basis, it's a good idea to take along a bathrobe and a pair of bedroom slippers.

The price we give for meals includes one drink, appetizer, entrée, and dessert per person, not including tips.

1 Chesapeake Region

2 West Virginia

3 Tidewater Virginia

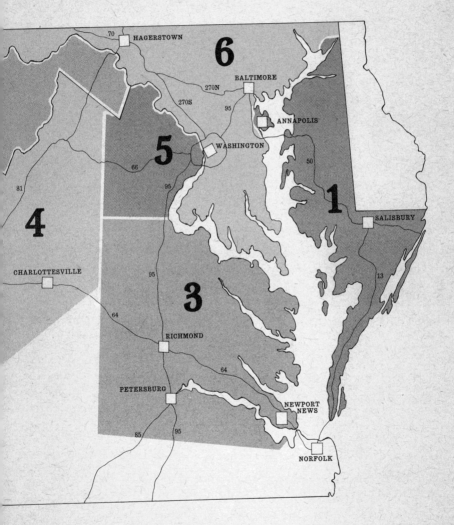

4   **Shenandoah Virginia**

5   **Northern Virginia**

6   **Mainland Maryland**

CHESAPEAKE REGION

MARYLAND & VIRGINIA

If this were an animal, it'd be a crab. An isolated maritime world with customs and traditions that have been carried over almost unchanged for the past 250 years, the Chesapeake section is a world in itself. The eastern shore of Maryland and Virginia, bounded by the Chesapeake Bay on the west and the Atlantic Ocean on the east, is as different from the rest of the two states as the colonial United States was from Britain. In fact, it is often jokingly referred to as the overseas colonies.

Annapolis is the gateway to this Chesapeake section. From November 26, 1783, until August 13, 1784, Annapolis was the capital of the country, and it's still the capital of Maryland. The historic town, home of The Naval Academy, provides hours worth of sightseeing and shopping.

The rest of the Chesapeake section is reached by crossing the Chesapeake Bay Bridge from Annapolis. You'll find the picturesque communities of St. Michaels and Oxford (the Oxford-Bellvue ferry, the oldest continuously operating ferry in the country, provides a shortcut between these two towns). St. Michaels is the site of the beautiful lighthouse you always see in Maryland promotional material. The lighthouse is now the Chesapeake Bay Maritime Museum, filled with maritime memorabilia from belaying pins to entire ships. Adjacent is a waterfowl museum filled with exhibits of mounted waterfowl and interpretative exhibits of hunting on the peninsula. Hunting is big sport here, since it is on the duck and goose migration route.

Along the Atlantic coast of the peninsula lies a string of barrier islands. The Maryland islands, for the most part, are heavily developed. But little Smith and Tangier islands are quaint, unspoiled places, where the residents still retain the accents of their Cornish ancestors. And further south are Assateague Island National Seashore (a 37-mile-long island that reaches into Maryland and Virginia), which is still untouched by resort development, and Chincoteague, where the biggest event is the annual auction of the wild ponies that swim over from Assateague. Also nearby is the Wallops Island facility of the National Aeronautics & Space Administration; if you're lucky you might be there for the launching of a rocket. Theirs are mostly weather or research rockets, but the fireworks are just as spectacular as those lifted off from Cape Canaveral.

The rest of the islands on the Virginia end are unspoiled wilderness thanks to the efforts of the nature Conservancy, a private group that set up a dummy real estate development corporation and bought up all of the land, ostensibly to build more condominiums. After all the land was bought, the group announced its plans to manage the islands as areas for hikers and backpackers.

July is the month for seafood festivals around the area, with the biggest being in Ocean City, Maryland. Labor Day means Skipjack races on Deal Island, and October brings Chesapeake Appreciation days.

And of course, the seafood fan will go wild in this area. Fresh crabs, oysters, clams are served everywhere—and anyone from the Chesapeake Bay area can tell you that nothing tops their fresh seafood.

CHANNEL BASS INN
CHINCOTEAGUE, VA.

The day ended with a torrent of sunlight, which filled the sea and flowed among the islets and clumps of marsh grass that formed a bridge between Chincoteague Island and the Virginia mainland.

Downtown Chincoteague is a strip of highway lined with shops that cater to the summer floods of people. The town is much more relaxed when the summer visitors are gone—there is not even a reminder of the mobs that packed the sidewalks only a few months before.

Chincoteague is delightful during its off-season. One of the things that makes it so enjoyable is the Channel Bass Inn, a cozy place with owners/innkeepers who enjoy making their guests feel welcome and comfortable. Although it is a disappointment to find the inn located across the street from a gas station instead of right on the water, any sense of disappointment fades once you go inside.

Like so many inns, the Channel Bass was formerly a rambling single-family home with enough bedrooms for a huge family and enough gables to keep a novelist busy for at least three books. The front porch is an ideal relaxation spot in the summer, although it is a bit chilly in the winter. The inn is about five miles from the beach.

Jim and Cathy Hanretta bought the Channel Bass Inn after all of eight hours reflection and with no experience

ADDRESS: Chincoteague, Virginia 23336. Take Route 175 from Route 13 on the Delmarva Peninsula. When 175 dead ends into the main street of Chincoteague, turn left and drive about four blocks to Church Street (there's an Arco gas station on the corner), turn right; The Channel Bass Inn will be on the right, just one building from the corner
TELEPHONE: 804-336-6148
FACILITIES: Ten rooms with shared baths; dining during the winter on Friday, Saturday, and Sunday from 6 to 9:30 p.m., and for breakfast on Saturday and Sunday from 9 to 11 a.m. Open full time during the summer; call ahead to confirm hours
RATES: $20 per night for either singles or doubles
RESERVATIONS: Required
DRESS: Whatever you want to wear short of bare feet, but you would not feel out of place with a coat for dinner
CREDIT CARDS: American Express, Master Charge

in running an inn. One thing for sure, their lack of experience doesn't show at all.

Jim kicked around Europe for several years, earning his meals by playing the guitar in restaurants, *pensions,* and inns, and he became intrigued by what went on in the kitchen. He has brought together what he learned from many of the great chefs of Europe and from the love of Spanish food he developed when his family lived in Peru. The result is a unique style of cuisine that makes the Channel Bass Inn one of the best restaurants anywhere.

His meals are built around four of his own sauces— Espagnol and Provençal are the primary ones, with a Continental sauce and a red Peruvian sauce supplementing them.

Illustrative of his care in preparing even side dishes is the rice, in which Jim uses saffron, despite its difficulty to obtain and its expense. The use of the highest quality ingredients and the enormous amount of effort expended on each dish make the food expensive—not expensive as restaurants go, but more expensive than most country inns. We spent $35 for an evening meal for two that started with an apéritif, followed by our entrées (trout stuffed with crabmeat for me, shrimp Provençal for Shan), saffron rice, a Spanish salad (cucumber, tomato, and green peppers, no lettuce), and dessert with coffee. It was well worth the price.

Besides being friendly, the service was very attentive.

We were not rushed through any of our courses, but we didn't have to wait a long time between courses either. There were a lot of extra touches—the sourdough bread with its tart aftertaste, the delicate dressing on the salad, German chocolate cake that was *sehr wunderbar,* fresh flowers on tables that are not jammed together.

And the chef/owner provided the final touch. Jim learned flamenco and Spanish guitar in Barcelona, and after he finished preparing the last order (about 10 p.m. or thereafter) he came into the dining room and performed for his guests.

The overnight accommodations at the Channel Bass Inn are simple but very comfortable and tastefully decorated. Antiques dominate the décor, supplemented by original art on the walls. Most of the rooms are on a share-a-bath basis, with a sink in the rooms.

Tourists come to Chincoteague primarily in the summer to enjoy the sun, sand, and surf and to mingle with all of the other people who have showed up to do the same thing. The annual roundup of the wild ponies is another attraction that draws people here, although it has recently come under attack by environmentalists.

CHESAPEAKE HOUSE, MRS. CROCKETT'S
TANGIER ISLAND, VA.

Although Tangier Island was discovered in 1608 by Captain John Smith of Pocahontas fame, it wasn't settled until about 1650 when a man named West (first name lost to posterity) persuaded the Indians to sell him the island for two overcoats.

The island cost a bit more than the blanket that Manhatten went for, but look what's here ... and what is not here. There are about 1,000 people, lots of fishing boats, little narrow streets filled with bicycles, a wildlife preserve, and the Chesapeake Bay all around. What's not here are cars, crime, noise, urban problems, and smog.

The island is a perfect place for relaxing, strolling, enjoying the scenery, and getting to know a closed culture that has grown different by staying the same, isolated from modern civilization.

Mrs. Crockett's Chesapeake House is the only place to eat or stay overnight on the island. But it plays to packed crowds because it is so good. I can't think of a better way to describe Tangier and Mrs. Crockett's than to include this entry from the travel diary of a close friend, Doris Wagley, who visited there recently with her son, Christian.

We arrived in Crisfield and missed the tour boat to Tangier Island. We ate in a cafe near the city dock and asked about other transportation. The gal suggested we talk with Roger Evans, who lives on Tangier. Roger had just brought in his

ADDRESS: Tangier Island, Virginia 23440
TELEPHONE: 804-891-2331
FACILITIES: 7 rooms with shared bath. Dining daily from
6:30 a.m. to 6 p.m.
RATES: American plan (breakfast and dinner included with
room) costs $18 per day per person. Meals only, $5.95 per
person including tax and gratuity
RESERVATIONS: Required
DRESS: Casual
CREDIT CARDS: None

day's catch of crabs and was eating lunch before returning to
Tangier. He invited us to go back to the island with him and
his son; we accepted.

Mrs. Crockett's Chesapeake House is the only place on the
island with overnight accommodations. We arrived at about
3:45, got off Roger's boat, and asked directions. We dragged
suitcase and beach gear a couple of blocks down to Mrs. Crockett's; they had room for us that night. This was a Wednesday
afternoon. Our room was upstairs and had two double beds and
a single bed in it. Weekdays they generally don't fill up with
people; weekends you must make reservations in advance. We
went out to find bicycles; went over to the airport at the other
end of the island from Mrs. Crockett's and rented an adult bike
and a kid's bike for $2 each for a 24-hour period. Rode the bikes
back to Mrs. Crockett's. At 5, dinner was called and we ate all
we wanted, family style, of clam fritters, peas, potato salad, cole
slaw, apple sauce, homemade bread, ham, two each (the limit)
of crab cakes, corn pudding, homemade pound cake, iced tea (no
alcoholic beverages served).

The downstairs part of Mrs. Crockett's is practically all
kitchen and dining rooms. Upstairs are rooms with one large
bathroom; across the street is another guest house with bathroom but no eating facilities. Our room was very clean; the ice
bucket was filled and the glasses were wrapped in plastic bags
from their kitchen.

Houses on the island are generally small and generally very
well kept. All houses near the docks (this appears to be the
part that was built on first) have fenced yards; graves are
seen in many of the yards. Everyone has a bike; mothers have
babies in the front baskets of the bikes, with pillows in the
baskets.

The children were polite and generally friendly. The adults
were friendly also and spoke with a cockney-type accent (they
are actually of Cornish ancestry).

The fishermen and crabbers are up at 4 a.m. all but Sunday
mornings to go out for their catch. They take their day's catch
to Crisfield at about noon and return to Tangier. Some work on
their boats until dinner at 5.

No movie theaters; no supermarkets, only a few small grocery
stores.

There are two churches on the island—Methodist and one

similar to Methodist. The people are generally quite religious (all 950 of them), generally do not drink alcoholic beverages. Sunday is their Sabbath and they don't work the waters.

Lots of canals run through the island—footbridges accommodate bikes and the one pickup truck I saw, which is used for deliveries and trash pickups. One church has a Volkswagen van. One road all around the island is wide enough to carry the motor vehicles; other streets near the houses are very narrow and only accommodate bikes.

The airport can accommodate up to eighty airplanes on busy Sundays.

As darkness approaches, everyone goes inside and by about 10 p.m. most of the lights are out. We waited turns for showers and visited with other guests. No radio and no TV at Mrs. Crockett's. After you bicycle for several hours and eat all that food, you're ready for bed at 10. Before leaving after the dinner clean-up, Mrs. Crockett's daughters (who now run the house since Mrs. Crockett's recent death) learn who needs to be awakened to catch the 8 a.m. mail boat the next morning. There was an exhaust fan in the floor of our room about 12" in diameter, through which we could see the kitchen below. At about 7 a.m. I awakened to the clatter of pans, the smell of homemade bread and fresh coffee. What a great way to wake up! When we arrived for breakfast, we were given juice and coffee, a platter of bacon and homemade bread. Eggs were cooked as we requested; breakfast was delicious.

Mrs. Crockett's can be reached from either Maryland or Virginia. The mail boat leaves Crisfield, Maryland, each afternoon at 12:30 p.m. (except Sundays, October through May) and takes about an hour and ten minutes to arrive. It leaves for its return trip at 8 a.m. the next morning. A private boat, the *Steven Thomas,* is also available. For details contact Captain Rudy Thomas (reservations required, 804-891-2240). Rides with fishermen who live on Tangier are also available at times.

From Virginia's Northern Neck, a cruiseship, the *Captain Thomas,* departs Reedville at 10 a.m. and returns at 4 p.m. Contact Captain Stanley Bowis (reservations required, 703-333-4656). There is also a small airstrip for private airplanes.

CHESAPEAKE HOUSE
TILGHMAN, MD.

If you're looking for a rustic place on the bay, if you like to fish, and if you like a place that has the atmosphere of a family café in small-town America, The Chesapeake House on Tilghman Island is the place. It is neither a sophisticated nor a romantic place. But it's a lot of fun, whether you go for a casual evening meal or to spend a weekend fishing and relaxing.

The rambling Chesapeake House at Dogwood Harbor has been a favorite spot with fishermen for more than half a century. Levin Harrison, Sr., the inn's owner, chartered his first fishing boat in 1910 and is still going strong, though his son, Levin, Jr., is now the skipper of their fishing operation. The Chesapeake House has a twelve-boat charter fleet, each of which rents for $125 per day, tackle included.

The dining room is decorated in early American Legion—knotty pine walls and all the appropriate nautical wall decorations. But under all the simplicity and small-town atmosphere, there is a very good chef, a wine list that would do justice to many urban restaurants, and a menu selection that includes a superb cream of crab soup and one of the widest selections of seafood anywhere on the bay. There are also a number of meat dishes for the non-fish lover. Platters of vegetables are served family

ADDRESS: Tilghman, Maryland 21671, on Route 33 south of St. Michaels
TELEPHONE: 301-886-2123
FACILITIES: 32 rooms with shared baths, 16 rooms with private baths. Dining daily from 6 a.m. to 10 p.m. Closed November to April
RATES: Room rates, with all meals included, are $12.50 per night per person on weekdays, $29 per person for the entire weekend
RESERVATIONS: Not necessary for meals; required for lodgings
DRESS: Casual to blue jeans
CREDIT CARDS: None

style.

The rambling old house has thirty-two rooms, none with private baths. There is also a more modern, motelish unit nearby that has about half as many rooms, all with private baths. The interior decorating of the rooms is undistinguished; the food is the big attraction here.

GRATITUDE LANDING
ROCK HALL, MD.

The steamboats don't stop in Rock Hall anymore. And nobody seems to know what happened to the *S.S. Gratitude,* which served this spit of land in the Chesapeake Bay for more than three decades during the late 1800's and early 1900's, and for which a bustling port in Rock Hall was named. The *S.S. Gratitude* was sold to Cuban owners in 1914, and its history seems to have ended there.

The port of Gratitude, which is in the small crabbing and fishing hamlet of Rock Hall, played an important role during the Revolutionary War. Patriots from the southern colonies, including George Washington, Jefferson, and the Lee family, followed a route to Philadelphia for meetings of the Continental Congress that took them by land through Virginia and Maryland to the port of Annapolis. In Annapolis they boarded a ferry that crossed the bay to Rock Hall, where they continued their journey to Philadelphia.

The ferry that these founding fathers took was owned and operated by Horatio Middleton, an Annapolis tavern owner (see Middleton Tavern, page 16). He started the ferry service in 1768 and became well known both for his fine food and lodgings and for the service of the ferry. Today, there is again a connection between Annapolis and

ADDRESS: Rock Hall, Maryland 21661. Take Route 20 through Rock Hall
TELEPHONE: 301-639-7064
FACILITIES: Dining only, open April through October; Wednesday through Monday from noon to 10 p.m. Saturday and Sunday brunches are served buffet style from 8 to 11 a.m., and a special buffet seafood dinner served from 5:30 to 10 p.m. Fridays
RESERVATIONS: Not necessary, except during the summer
DRESS: Casual
CREDIT CARDS: BankAmericard and Master Charge

Rock Hall. Jerry Hardesty, who restored the Middleton Tavern to its original function as an old-time ordinary, now operates the small inn at Gratitude, which sits smack at the edge of the water. There is no longer a ferry, but the inn is surrounded now by pleasure boats and by the oyster and crab fishermen who can often be observed from the windows in the main dining room.

As with Hardesty's other enterprise, Gratitude Landing has no overnight accommodations, though they are available a short walk away (see Shady Rest, page 27).

Inside, Gratitude Landing looks like the dining salon of a tall windjammer: lots of varnished wood, nautical paraphernalia, and a view of water and ships from every window, giving one the impression of being afloat.

We sat at a corner table from which we could see the boats anchored nearby and out into the bay to a landless horizon. The meal started with cheese and crackers, and a basket filled with hot homemade bread formed into rather flat, oval-shaped buns, brown and flaky. My crab cakes were two solid masses of sweet crabmeat with hardly any filling at all, and instead of being deep fried were sautéed in butter. They were superb. Likewise, the fried shrimp Shan ordered were tender and fresh, but not greasy. The cole slaw was creamy, and the potatoes accompanying the meal were cooked together with onions and green peppers in a bit of bacon fat. The cook/manager, Ernie Keywater, calls them Parisian potatoes.

Unless you are used to mineral-tasting water, don't drink the water or order iced tea or coffee. The iron is overpowering.

Our meal cost us $15 with tip.

MARYLAND INN
ANNAPOLIS, MD.

The sky was fading and only the stragglers had yet to finish furling their sails in the Old Town Annapolis harbor when we arrived at the Maryland Inn on Church Circle. We walked across the front porch (where lunch and cocktails are served in warm weather) and into the cozy lobby with its marble floors, tall ceilings, and period furnishings.

There are only forty-four rooms here, and the desk clerks usually know you by name when you arrive. We registered and were handed two room keys.

"Go take a look at both of these and take the one you like best," she told us. Her assistant behind the desk told us that one of the rooms, number 401, was her favorite. It was ours too, with a large sweeping curve instead of one corner, a magnificently crafted bedside table with intricate marquetry, and period furnishings that ran the gamut from Queen Anne to Louis XIV. The room is marred somewhat by the presence of a color television and the incessant murmur of the window unit air conditioner, but these are minor indeed when stacked against the regal high ceilings and the eighteen-inch-thick masonry walls.

The Maryland Inn has operated continuously since the 1770's when it was built by an Annapolis merchant named Thomas Hyde. It originally had twenty-two rooms

ADDRESS: Church Circle, Annapolis, Maryland 21401. Take the Naval Academy Exit from Route 50. This road, West Street, leads directly to Church Circle

TELEPHONE: 301-263-2641

FACILITIES: 44 rooms with private baths, TV's. Special holiday rates; swimming, tennis, sailing, and sailing lessons can be arranged through the front desk. Breakfast from 7:30 to 11 a.m. weekdays, 8 to 11 a.m. Saturdays, and Sunday brunch from 8 a.m. to 1:30 p.m. Lunch from 11:30 to 3 p.m. Monday through Saturday. Dinner from 6 to 10 p.m. weekdays, until 11 p.m. Saturdays, and 3:30 to 9 p.m. Sundays

RESERVATIONS: Required

DRESS: Nice casual in the day, informal at night

CREDIT CARDS: American Express, BankAmericard, Master Charge

and was three-stories tall. Built between two spokes of streets leading into Church Circle, the building has a flatiron shape when viewed from above. The fourth story and the ornamental porches were added about 100 years ago.

The Treaty of Paris, ending the War for Independence, was signed just a block away from here in 1784, and historians say that it's likely that many of the signers and participants stayed at the inn.

The desk clerk graciously made dinner reservations for us at the inn's Treaty of Paris restaurant, and after putting our suitcases in the room we walked down the stairs to eat.

The low-ceilinged room with fireplaces at each end has a colonial atmosphere. Although for breakfast the next morning we would sit by the smaller of the two fireplaces, that night we sat in front of the larger one, which contained a display of open-fire cooking instruments.

We started dinner with a house specialty that ought to win a medal: crabmeat bisque, a hearty, creamy dish filled with nuggets of backfin crab in a fish stock. The spinach salad tossed at the table with just a hint of the house dressing was nearly as wonderful. From the baby flounder stuffed with crabmeat to the seafood crêpes, care and quality of preparation was apparent.

The Treaty offers a good wine list, complete with labels from each of the wines so that you can select a favorite by brand as well as by vintage, varietal, or region. The wine list also gives a recommended wine for each dish on the menu.

The restaurant staff was extremely courteous and friendly. Our meal came to about $35 for two.

After finishing dessert we walked back to the room to find that the desk clerks had apparently spotted us for newlyweds, for on our dresser was a bottle of champagne in a bucket of ice (we've actually been married for six years). I called down to the desk to explain the mistake and was told, "go ahead and enjoy it. Anybody that has been married that long and enjoys it that much deserves to celebrate."

A great way to end the evening is to go to The King of France Tavern, located downstairs next to The Treaty of Paris. It offers great jazz in an eighteenth-century tavern. Regular performers include Charlie Byrd and Earl "Fatha" Hines.

The Maryland Inn is a perfect base for walking excursions of Annapolis. The old state capitol is a block away, and the Naval Academy is only about a fifteen-minute walk. The Annapolis Market in the middle of old town is a fascinating place to visit for fresh fruits and vegetables, candies, unusual foods, crafts, and a raw oyster bar where you eat them as the man shucks them.

Working crab boats, charter boats, and spectacular pleasure yachts are moored at the dock, and it's a treat to just walk around and inspect them.

For people who like a bit of structure in their sight-seeing, guided tours are available from the nonprofit Historic Annapolis Organization, which will take you around to such local landmarks as the Brice House, Paca House, and the famous Hammond-Harwood House, all over 200 years old.

MIDDLETON TAVERN
ANNAPOLIS, MD.

Although the ferry that Horatio Middleton operated no longer connects Annapolis with Maryland's Eastern Shore, his tavern still stands and today is as much a favorite with the Maryland state legislators as it was originally with the founding fathers. The Middleton Tavern, sitting smack in the middle of old town Annapolis, was a favorite spot with members of the Continental Congress, who met at the nearby statehouse to sign the Treaty of Paris. According to the inn's present owners, George Washington, Benjamin Franklin, and Thomas Jefferson were among those who frequented the tavern. Built around 1740, the tavern was originally known as an "Inn for Sea Faring Men."

After his death, Horatio Middleton's tavern was operated by relatives and finally by John Randall, Annapolis' mayor in the early 1800's, revolutionary logistics officer, and partner in the architectural firm that designed the famous Hammond-Harwood House. President James Monroe visited the tavern both while he was President and before then, when he was a delegate to the Continental Congress.

The inn went through a succession of owners during the twentieth century, serving as a rooming house of little distinction until its purchase by the present owners in

ADDRESS: 2 Market Place, Annapolis, Maryland 21401
TELEPHONE: 301-263-3323
FACILITIES: Dining only, lunch from 11:30 a.m. to 3:30 p.m., dinner served downstairs from 5 to 10:30 p.m. and upstairs from 6 to 10 p.m.
RESERVATIONS: Recommended
DRESS: Casual downstairs and at sidewalk tables; a coat is recommended for the upstairs dining room
CREDIT CARDS: BankAmericard and Master Charge

1968.

Today, the building is a registered historic landmark, but serious fires in the past have destroyed much of the original interior of the Georgian brick structure. Therefore, although the outside has been restored in keeping with its historical vintage, the inside is colonial Holiday Inn design, with fire-engine red wallpaper and spindle dividers that visually overpower the only remaining guardian of history, the stone fireplace.

But the lack of historical atmosphere, luckily, does not overshadow the food and the service. The restaurant's luncheon menu runs heavily to egg and crêpe dishes, although a mix of American, French, and Italian entrées are offered. The food is plentiful and well prepared; the service is friendly if not always prompt. The crab crêpes may win the hearts of many, but the restaurant's forte is its sauces—Bordelaise, hollandaise, Béarnaise, and mushroom—which are made by the chef and are available à la carte with any course. Second only to the sauces is the variety of desserts, from bananas flambé to strawberries *zabaglione*. The coffee is good. The waiters wear breeches and knee socks, but the background music is folk-country-western Muzak.

The Middleton Tavern is not an inexpensive place to eat. A lunch for two (consisting of an order of eggs Benedict, an omelette Espanol, and coffee) ran $12. The Tavern includes a 20 percent service charge with the price of the meal.

MRS. KITCHING'S
SMITH ISLAND, MD.

All 750 people on Smith Island, Maryland's only community accessible solely by boat, are direct descendants of the original settlers from England and Cornwall who settled here in 1657. They didn't need much in the way of public services then and they don't today. No big government for these people; in fact, there's no government at all—no governing body, no police, and no jails.

"Supply and demand," said one resident. "We got enough bureaucrats and politicians bothering us from the state and U.S.; don't need the home-grown variety. No jails? Well sir, if we'd a needed 'em, we'd 'a got 'em."

We left Crisfield at half past noon on the *Betty Jo Tyler*, a cruise boat that is the only way to make an afternoon trip out of a visit to the island. The only other way to get there is to take the mail boat, which doesn't return until the next day.

The *Betty Jo* is named after the daughter of Captain Alan Tyler, who lives at Rhodes Point, one of the three small settlements on the island. The other two settlements are Ewell and Tylerton.

We docked at the pier in Ewell and boarded a small school bus for a tour of the island. Roads are so narrow that, if the bus had had one more coat of paint on it, we

ADDRESS: Mrs. Frances Kitching, Smith Island, Ewell,
Maryland 21824
TELEPHONE: 301-425-3321
FACILITIES: 4 rooms, with shared bath. Dining daily;
breakfast, lunch, and dinner served about 8 a.m., noon, and
6 p.m. respectively, or whenever a group of people has made a
prior reservation to eat
RATES: $16 per person for double room, including evening
meal and breakfast
RESERVATIONS: If you take the Betty Jo Tyler, Capt. Tyler
will make reservations for you to eat about 2 p.m. Otherwise,
prior reservations for food or lodgings are required
DRESS: Casual
CREDIT CARDS: None. Cash preferred, though checks are
taken

would have been in an accident. Fig trees and pomegranate bushes were in evidence everywhere. We had come
a bit late for the figs, but the limbs of the pomegranate
bushes were bent low by the weight of the funny-looking
fruits.

The bus dropped us off in front of Mrs. Kitching's
white frame building. Besides serving food, she has four
rooms (share a bath) for overnight guests.

Those who did not get off the bus to eat with us were
sorry afterwards. We were served homemade tomato
bisque soup that was thick and creamy, followed by maca-
roni salad, a carrot and onion salad, chicken and broccoli
casserole, crab cakes, corn custard casserole, green beans,
rolls, all topped off by a custardy sweet potato pie. Everything is served family style, with four to twelve people at
a table. All the while Mrs. Kitching is fluttering from table
to table (there are five) along with her helper to make sure
serving dishes are full, that you're enjoying the food,
that your glass is filled. And if you don't have seconds,
you're going to hurt her feelings. The meals cost $6 per
person.

We decided to walk around the island before the boat
returned, and so for about an hour we explored the narrow streets, the general store, and we talked with many
of the residents of Ewell, who were about as friendly as
people come. Unlike Tangier Island, where every house is
surrounded by a chain link fence and has a family graveyard in the front yard, there were few fences here. There

was an ordinary graveyard by the church, and cats everywhere you looked. The feline population must outnumber the people by two to one. There's not as much to see or explore here as there is on Tangier Island, but because of this there are fewer tourists to make things crowded.

To get to Smith Island, either take the mail boat, which leaves Crisfield at noon every day except Sunday, or take the *Betty Jo Tyler* (call Capt. Tyler, 301-425-2771, for information). The *Betty Jo* doesn't run at times during the winter, so it's best to call ahead before planning to take the day trip, which starts at Somers Cove Marina in Crisfield at 12:30 p.m. and returns about five hours later. The boat is $8 a person, children half price.

THE PASADENA
ROYAL OAK, MD.

Fred Harper would have liked the Pasadena. Well, that is to say, Fred Harper still does like the Pasadena, even though he has been dead for more than half a century. Fred lives in the fifth floor of the mammoth plantation house and takes care to shut the windows when it rains, and does little odd jobs like fixing up wallpaper. Fred, according to those who know him, is a good ghost.

Parts of the massive white-columned house are nearly 250 years old, and during his ownership of it and the 3,000 acres of land, Fred Harper put his nine sons and daughters to work enlarging and expanding, adding and embellishing, so that when he died in the 1920's it was a house big enough to use as an inn.

The story has it that Fred's ghost came back because he was disturbed at the house being allowed to fall into disrepair and at the land being sold parcel by parcel. He was also disturbed that none of his nine offspring had any children of their own, and that there was, therefore, no heir to inherit the Pasadena.

But since its purchase about seven years ago by a German cultural exchange organization, Schwaben International, there hasn't been that much for Fred Harper to do. The building has been put into excellent repair and

ADDRESS: Route 329, Royal Oak, Maryland 21662. Take Route 33 from Easton to Route 329

TELEPHONE: 301-745-2288

FACILITIES: 40 rooms, some in cabins, some with private baths. Closed November 15-April 1 since it has no heat. Breakfast served from 8:30 to 9:30 a.m., lunch from noon to 1 p.m., dinner from 5:30 to 6:30 p.m.

RATES: Modified American Plan (breakfast and dinner included in price of room). Rates range from $15 per day per person (double occupancy) for a room without private bath during the off-season, to $19.50 a day per person (double occupancy) for a private bath during their season (June 1 to Sept. 30)

RESERVATIONS: Required for lodgings. Meals available only for overnight guests unless you call at least a day ahead

DRESS: Nice casual

CREDIT CARDS: Master Charge

the grounds—the remaining 135 acres of Harper's estate —are now well kept. Members of the cultural exchange organization use it as a conference center, but you don't have to be a member to stay here. In fact, the only hints that this is something other than a beautiful country inn are the brochures telling you so and an occasional copy of *Stern* magazine on a table or chair.

Rooms are comfortable and furnished mostly with American antiques or reproductions. There are a total of forty rooms, some in cabins, a few with private baths. The only problem with the rooms in the main house are the solid oak floors that creak at the lightest touch.

The feeling of amity among guests at the Pasadena is extraordinary and due in large part to the gregariousness of Mickey McCrea, the inn's resident manager, maintenance man, chief cook, bottle washer, lawn keeper, maître d', and social director. Mickey passes through the public rooms like a hurricane of humor and conversation; guests find themselves making friends and talking to people they've never seen before. The new friendships are reenforced by the family-style dinners at tables seating six to ten people. The dining room overlooks the boathouse on the Miles River, which is part of the Pasadena's backyard.

The family-style meals are a delight, with the tables piled high with serving bowls full of fresh vegetables and a variety of homecooked meals, chicken, or fish. Seconds are allowable and taken frequently.

The Pasadena has a swimming pool. Golf, tennis, and horseback riding are available nearby. The town of Royal Oak consists of the Pasadena, an old general store, a one-room post office, and an antique/junk store, which piles up its items for sale on both sides of the narrow road that winds through the block-long town. The store also has two buildings crammed with furniture and odd artifacts, which makes for some interesting rummaging although prices tend to be high.

The fall is a fine time to visit, since you can see the ducks and geese migrating south. The nearby picturesque village of St. Michaels, with its Chesapeake Bay Maritime Museum and Waterfowl Museum, is only a short bicycle ride away. And the Tred Avon Ferry to Oxford is a short car ride away. Oxford has many fine antique shops, as well as one of the most famous inns in the area, the Robert Morris Inn.

ROBERT MORRIS INN
OXFORD, MD.

Oxford had been a thriving colonial port for more than 100 years when the Declaration of Independence was signed. It was one of Maryland's official ports of entry, and by the middle of the eighteenth century rivaled Annapolis as the busiest port in all of Maryland. Today, Oxford is a sleepy, picturesque hamlet —located on the peninsula bounded by the Tred Avon River and Town Creek—whose biggest excitement is the frequent arrival of the Oxford-Bellvue ferry loaded with all of six autos and an occasional pedestrian or bicycle rider. Historians claim that this is the oldest ferry crossing in the country, dating from 1683. The ferry is the quickest and most enjoyable route between Oxford and St. Michaels. From May 1 to Labor Day, it makes its run across the narrow river from 7 a.m. to 9 p.m. Monday through Thursday, until 11 p.m. Fridays, 9 a.m. to 11 p.m. Saturdays, and 9 a.m. to 9 p.m. Sundays. Winter hours vary and are posted on the piers at both sides of the river.

One nice thing about the ferry is that it lets you off in Oxford right at the side of the Robert Morris Inn. The Robert Morris Inn was built about 1710, some say earlier, by ship's carpenters, whose nautical skills constructed a seaworthy and stout, yet graceful, structure using wooden

ADDRESS: Oxford, Maryland 21654. Take Route 333 from Easton and follow it to the Bellevue Ferry. Or, from St. Michaels, head toward Royal Oak and follow signs to the Bellevue Oxford Ferry

TELEPHONE: 301-226-5111

FACILITIES: 29 rooms, 25 of which have shared baths. Closed from mid-January to the first week in March. No pets. Breakfast served from 8:30 to 11 a.m., lunch from 11:30 a.m. to 4 p.m., and dinner from 5 to 9 p.m.

RATES: Prices range from $19.76 to $35.26

RESERVATIONS: Required

DRESS: Nice casual

CREDIT CARDS: American Express, BankAmericard, Master Charge

pegged paneling, ship's nails, hand-hewn beams, and wide plank floors. The details of the old-time quality construction can be seen on the inside, from the handmade nails and paneling to the fireplaces in four of the guest rooms, which are constructed of brick that was used as ballast on the sailing ships as they made their trips from England across the Atlantic.

Robert Morris, Sr., was a successful merchant from Liverpool who came to Oxford in 1783 and built a large and well-known shipping and mercantile business. His son, Robert, Jr., who was to become known as "the Financier of the Revolution," came to America some ten years later when he was apprenticed to a mercantile firm in Philadelphia (in which he later became a partner). The firm, Willing and Morris, acted as the purchasing agent for the Continental Congress. As a member of this body, Robert, Jr., was one of the signers of the Declaration of Independence.

While others were afraid to risk money on the radical idea of a new American nation, Robert, Jr., spent his entire savings as Superintendent of Finance for the Continental Congress and as a result became close friends of General George Washington. Robert, Jr., was an enormously powerful man in the crucial years of 1780 and 1781, but he died a poor man as the result of bad judgment in land speculation.

Robert Morris, Sr., had died an ironic death in 1750, when he was struck by the wadding from a ship's cannon that was fired in the harbor as a salute in his honor.

Morris, Sr., lived in the house that is now the inn from his arrival in Oxford until his death. The building has undergone several expansions since the original structure was built, but none have detracted from its unique construction and charming atmosphere.

The tavern, with its brick fireplace, low ceilings, and warm wood walls, is a favorite place for diners. When we arrived for lunch it was a nippy Saturday morning in March, and a fire gave warmth to the hearth and a glow to the diners, who were mostly dressed in their tweeds, leathers, and other clothing that could be described as country gentry casual. Evenings are dressier, with a coat and tie preferred.

We were settled in by our host at a cozy table for two in a corner. As people may tell you, Maryland is for crabs, and the Robert Morris serves some of the best. Although seafood is featured on the menu we found their beef dishes equally well prepared and the omelettes a delight. The Mocha Cream Cake was worth a trip to the inn itself.

Take a walk around the village and observe the old homes dating from the eighteenth century, antique shops, the marinas, and Tred Avon Yacht Club. A walk down to the Robert Morris Lodge, a block away from the inn and across the street from the Yacht Club, is a rewarding experience. The lodge was built about 1876 and has been remodeled to accommodate the overflow lodgers from the inn.

The rooms at the inn are furnished with period pieces as much as possible, and are tastefully decorated with the décor unspoiled by hints of the Formica and plastic that dominate today's lodgings.

Oxford is very easy to reach by boat from the Chesapeake Bay by entering the Choptank River and following it to the Tred Avon River. There are excellent anchorages and marina facilities.

SHADY REST
ROCK HALL, MD.

The huge old white house with its enormous porch sits on the edge of the Chesapeake Bay, surrounded by apple trees and massive maples, and looks like what your favorite aunt's house should look like—comfortable, inviting, and big enough to handle all of the visiting relatives.

But instead of visiting relatives, Shady Rest in Rock Hall just has visitors who are treated like family in a down-home style that makes them relax.

Visitors enjoy playing bridge in the screened-in gazebo that would be under water if it were any closer to the bay, or just sitting on the front porch and relaxing, enjoying the stiff salt breezes while the insects thump and buzz their complaints about not being able to get in.

There's not much to do at Shady Rest. Perhaps that's why it's so popular with people who come here not to do things—not to engage in the manic activity that characterizes so many American vacations and leaves people more exhausted after than before. No, there's not much to do here and that has to be one of its greatest draws.

Mrs. Eulah Williams has operated Shady Rest since 1964 and has gained a reputation for fine food and comfortable lodgings. Most rooms do not have private baths, but their coziness and the presence of such home touches

ADDRESS: Rock Hall, Maryland 21661. Take Route 20 through Rock Hall until it dead ends into the Bay. Turn right at the last street before the dead end; Shady Rest will be on your left about 100 yards up this street

TELEPHONE: 301-639-2376

FACILITIES: 7 rooms; dining Monday through Saturday from 4 to 8 p.m., Sunday from 2 to 8 p.m. Closed from the end of October through Memorial Day, though it will re-open for any group of 15 people or more

RATES: $10 per night per person

RESERVATIONS: Required

DRESS: Casual

CREDIT CARDS: None, but personal checks are accepted

as handmade quilts and antique furnishings more than compensates for any inconvenience.

Dinner is the only meal that is served, but lunches and weekend brunches can be eaten at Gratitude Landing, about a three- to five-minute walk away. Dinners are served family style at a group of huge tables in the cozy dining room decorated by Mrs. Williams' plate collection. Seafood is the predominant dish, with fare ranging from sautéed shrimp and crab meat to crab cakes and a fish of the day. Steak and chicken lovers also have a variety to choose from, and it all tastes like a favorite aunt, who could cook, prepared it.

TIDEWATER INN
EASTON, MD.

The Tidewater Inn is one of those places that seems a lot smaller than it really is. It also seems a lot older than it really is. The cozy lobby is still used as such, with the readers of the Sunday *Times* seated on the overstuffed furniture next to departees waiting for the bellman, all taking occasional glances at new arrivals. A graceful curved staircase with a rubbed mahogany railing curves its way up from the lobby to the second floor. Although the Tidewater Inn is somewhat less than a half century old, the copious use of dark wood paneling and the careful planning of the décor gives it a decidedly mid-eighteenth century ambience.

Once you get past the lobby and the dining room, the beauty seems to fade into the mediocrity of Holiday Inn décor of the mid-1950's. The 125 rooms are comfortable, air conditioned, and have private baths and TV's, but there is little charming about them.

The town of Easton is filled with antique stores, small shops, and boutiques, which have sprung up largely due to the unusually large number of wealthy people who have settled in Easton and in Talbot County, of which Easton is the seat.

The outside of the Tidewater Inn is striking; it's all brick with a series of arched porticos along the front of

ADDRESS: P.O. Box 359, Easton, Maryland 21601
TELEPHONE: 301-822-1300
FACILITIES: 125 rooms, dining daily from 7 a.m. to 10 p.m.
RATES: Overnight accommodations for two plus dinner and brunch cost $50
RESERVATIONS: Recommended for food and lodging
DRESS: Nice casual during the day, formal at night
CREDIT CARDS: American Express, BankAmericard, Master Charge

the building, which faces the tree-shaded corner of Harrison and Dover Streets like the base of an equilateral triangle.

Fresh seafood from the local piers is the predominant item on the Tidewater's menu, although there is certainly a wide selection of beef and other meats. Sunday is my favorite time for eating here, for brunch or for Sunday dinner. A buffet style, unlimited-seconds brunch offers everything from eggs, bacon, sausage, and pancakes to chipped beef, homemade rolls, pastries, muffins, and more. Don't sleep too late, since things are apt to get quite crowded due to the brunch's popularity.

The Tidewater Inn has a swimming pool and offers tennis and golf at facilities nearby.

WASHINGTON HOTEL
PRINCESS ANNE, MD.

On June 8, 1928, a writer for the *New York World* said, "Maryland's fine cooking is almost non-existent; there are only three public eating places in the state where you can get a decent meal. Two of them are in Baltimore City; the other is in Princess Anne, a little town near the Virginia border where the Washington Hotel still remembers a high tradition." Today, there are many more than three places in Maryland where you can get a "decent meal," but the Washington Hotel still remembers the high tradition of which the New York writer wrote.

When that writer visited Princess Anne, it was a sleepy little tidewater town with narrow tree-lined streets, and the Washington Hotel stood by itself in a grove of elm trees. When this writer visited it, the town had evidently grown, though it is still sleepy by modern standards. Unfortunately, the town has not aged as gracefully as the hotel, for many of the trees have been replaced by an unplanned eyesore of garish signs and ugly buildings.

The hotel was established in 1744 and has been operated continuously since then, housing such personalities as Luther Martin, Maryland's first attorney general; several governors; and Samuel Chase, a signer of the Decla-

ADDRESS: Princess Anne, Maryland 21853. It is on the main street of Princess Anne, on your right as you come from Route 13
TELEPHONE: 301-651-2525; Mt. Vernon Inn, 301-651-3399
FACILITIES: 20 rooms; dining daily from 8 a.m. to 9 p.m. (bar open until 11:30 p.m.)
RATES: $15 for a double room
RESERVATIONS: Recommended for lodgings, not usually necessary for meals
DRESS: Casual
CREDIT CARDS: Hotel—BankAmericard; Restaurant—none, but takes personal checks

ration of Independence. Today's guests are more likely to be visiting professors from the nearby University of Maryland Eastern Shore campus and weekenders who use the hotel's central location to explore both shores of the peninsula.

Mrs. Mary Murphy and her husband operate the hotel, inherited from her parents. Mrs. Murphy says she has lived there for more than forty years now.

The front porch is furnished with weathered natural wood furniture, and the tiny entryway/lobby off the porch is just what you'd expect in a country hostel. Furnished with antiques and a collection of old pictures and newspaper clippings, it is cluttered and quaint. The staircase leading to the lodgings is a unique double one that was built, Mrs. Murphy told us, for the women in their hoop skirts to go up one side and the men to go up the other. At the top of the stairs is a magnificent, huge spinning wheel.

All of the twenty rooms have been remodeled and have private baths. The remodeling added comfort but failed to preserve any of the old-time atmosphere.

The dining room, known as the Mount Vernon Inn, is managed separately, although it's part of the same building. There are two rooms in which to eat, and you should request the old dining room. The other room, which is newer and not as nicely decorated, is okay for breakfast but not for a cozy evening meal.

The old dining room has a most unusual ceiling, which was built circa 1770 and consists of a series of dark wooden beams forming a series of squares. At every intersection of two beams is a dome-shaped section of a wooden ball to hide the joint. Our waitress said it was built by a Chinese cook for his mistress.

The dark wood on the ceiling is complemented by a red rubbed-brick fireplace that has a massive mantel, on which is hung an antique flintlock rifle. In one corner is an incredibly large corner cabinet, stretching from floor to high ceiling. The sideboard near our table was equally huge.

If you think their antiques are oversized, you should see the size of the meals. Any one item on my seafood platter—consisting of three soft-shelled crabs, about a dozen fried oysters, half a dozen shrimp, a huge crab cake, and an entire half of a large flounder—would have been a meal in itself. Shan ordered broiled lobster, which also came in an immense size.

The seafood was very fresh, and the entire meal enjoyable. We topped the meal off with freshly baked pie. Dinner for two with drinks and dessert was $21.

WEST VIRGINIA

West Virginia State Parks

Nobody goes anywhere in West Virginia in a straight line for long. The roads were built according to the spaghetti school of civil engineering, with serpentine curves and gerrymandered surfaces. If the authorities straightened out all the curves, there'd be enough left over to pave the entire state of Rhode Island and all the driveways in Chevy Chase.

The roads aren't much fun at night, but they wind through spectacular scenery and provide lots of areas to pull off and enjoy it. West Virginia's Eastern Panhandle is vast stretches of country dotted with tiny hamlets. Although unscrupulous strip mining companies have forever spoiled some of the scenery, most of it is wild, covered by a large portion of the Monongahela National Forest. There even are two wilderness areas, Dolly Sods and Otter Creek. The West Virginia state park system is the best in the country, and it's hard to go anywhere in the state without running across a state park or forest.

West Virginia is perfect for people seeking respite from the frenetic life. It offers activities ranging from civilized pursuits like golf and tennis to more rustic ones like backpacking and white-water rafting. Hunters, fishermen, and campers flock to the state, which is as wild and wonderful as its slogan boasts. And George Washington was just the first of many visitors who have come to enjoy the warm mineral springs at Berkeley Springs.

The Mountain Music Festival in Marlinton helps to perpetuate interest in the country folk music. Other festivals include the Petersburg White Water Weekend in April, and the Wildflower Festival at Blackwater Falls. Skiing in the wintertime, tours through the glass factories, and rides on the Cass Scenic Railroad are all things to enjoy in "the mountaineer state." You can even take a tour of a strip mine; there are several tours of deep tunnel mines in Beckley.

West Virginia was considered "the west" in the early days of our country, and its history is not as old as Maryland's or Virginia's. One exception is the restored village of Harper's Ferry, at the confluence of the Shenandoah and Potomac Rivers. It was here that John Brown's raid on the federal armory produced sparks that contributed to the start of the Civil War.

One of the best features of West Virginia is the low price of just about everything. Prices have increased considerably since the Depression, but the cost of meals and lodging often are half of what they would be in Washington.

BAVARIAN INN
SHEPHERDSTOWN, W. VA.

The sleepy, tree-lined hamlet of Shepherds-town, West Virginia, was spared by fate. Had the founding fathers decided differently, it might today be the site of the nation's capitol, for this was one of the sites favored by George Washington for building the new capitol. The small frontier town settled by people of German ancestry was a bustling place in Washington's time. In 1787 people lined the banks of the Potomac River there to see ''Crazy'' James Rumsey test out his steamboat, the Flying Teakettle. A monument to his success is located nearby for the lover of monuments to gaze upon.

Along with Shepherd's College, Shepherdstown has a formidable attraction in the Bavarian Inn. The town's German ancestry lives on inside the massive greystone mansion that was once the home of the town's wealthy mayor. Although built in this century, the impregnable-looking house definitely has a baronial air; only its lack of turrets and a moat prevent it from looking like a medieval castle.

But there's nothing forbidding about the Bavarian Inn—the inn overlooks grassy lawns just up the banks from the Potomac River and offers secluded dining insulated from the bustle of the highway by a forest of trees.

Inside the greetings are warm and heartily Germanic.

ADDRESS: Route 48, Shepherdstown, West Virginia 25443, just north of the Potomac Bridge
TELEPHONE: 304-876-6070
FACILITIES: Dining only; open year round, Monday, Wednesday, and Thursday from 6 p.m. to 2 a.m.; Friday, Saturday, and Sunday from 2 p.m. to 2 a.m. Closed Tuesdays
RESERVATIONS: Recommended
DRESS: Informal to dressy
CREDIT CARDS: American Express, BankAmericard, Master Charge

The substantial dark wood moldings and paneling give it a warm Bavarian Alp atmosphere that is cemented by a monstrous cuckoo clock in the entryway, whose grotesque dark wooden carvings of various game animals taken in a hunt reminds us that like many of our customs, the American hunting tradition is borrowed from another culture.

Hungarian immigrant and conversationalist supreme John Gradgel is the maître d', chief waiter, bartender, and entertainer whose thousands of stories, delivered in the most expressive and dramatic of tones and gestures, delight even the most jaded of listeners.

But despite his unique brand of entertainment and the décor distinguished only by the antique glass and china collection, the real attraction is the *wunderbar* Bavarian food—*wiener schnitzel, sauerbraten, bratwurst*—accompanied by sweet and sour red cabbage and potato dumplings. A Malfest is held in the spring and, of course, an Oktoberfest in the fall. Live Bavarian entertainment is featured at both these events. Dinner for two was $17.

BLACKWATER FALLS
DAVIS, W. VA.

Perhaps the best known of all the West Virginia state parks is the one at Blackwater Falls. The natural stone and wood lodge perches at the top of Blackwater River Gorge, and the whispering roar of the falls is an ever-present sound, even though they are nearly a mile away.

There is no golf course here (privileges available at Canaan Valley Resort), but the place is a swimmer's delight with both a "civilized" swimming pool and the more rustic Pendleton Lake. In the winter Pendleton Lake freezes over, and the surface is cleared of snow (the area receives more than 100 inches a year) to allow ice skating. Park Trails, along with trails in the nearby Monongahela National Forest, are ideal for cross-country skiing in the winter and hiking and backpacking in the summer. There is a wintertime sled run near the nature center.

The park naturalist and activities directors offer everything from nature hikes and wildflower tours to horseback riding (available within the park) and float and canoe trips. They can also put interested people in touch with private firms that give guided backpacking trips in the national forest, and its two close-in wilderness areas, Otter Creek and Dolly Sods.

ADDRESS: Davis, West Virginia 26260. The park entrance is a right turn as you head south on Route 32, just as you enter Davis

TELEPHONE: 304-259-5216

FACILITIES: State park and lodgings. 25 cabins, 65 tent and trailer campsites, some with hookups; 55 rooms in lodge, gift shop; dining is family style. Campsites and some of the cabins may have curtailed service in the winter

RATES: $16 for a single, $32 for 2 connecting rooms

RESERVATIONS: Required; the park is usually booked up two or three months in advance, and some favorite days in the summer are often booked as much as six months in advance

DRESS: Casual

CREDIT CARDS: BankAmericard

The park's hiking and nature trails are clearly marked and easy to use. The rhododendron trail is particularly beautiful when the flowers are blooming, usually in June. The rhododendron is the state flower and can be found in nearly every part of the state in a variety of hues, including purple, seldom seen anywhere else.

The sights of the Blackwater River gorge and falls can be enjoyed from a variety of vantage points. The overlook just in back of the lodge is a good place to start. Other overlooks include Pendleton Point on the other side of the gorge, from which you can see the lodge; the Elakala Falls overlook west of the lodge; and the overlook at Blackwater Falls. A mandatory trip is to walk the well-constructed wooden walkways and steps down at Blackwater to get a close-up view of the falls. The overlook at Pendleton Point is ideal for photographs of the sun as it sets in the long, craggy valley.

There are twenty-five cabins (for four, six, or eight people) and sixty-five tent and trailer campsites, some with hookups. The fifty-five rooms in the lodge are undistinguished, motel-type accommodations. There's a souvenir and gift shop at the lodge, but it carries mostly souvenir gimcracks in addition to toiletry items and magazines. The same can be said for the trading post near Blackwater Falls.

Food at Blackwater Falls Lodge is a country café menu with good ungarnished plain cooking in a family summer-camp atmosphere—high ceilings and linoleum tile floors that look like a marriage of ski lodge and YMCA. Dinner for two cost $9.

JIM BOLLINGER'S OAK SUPPER CLUB
PIPESTEM, W. VA.

Jim Bollinger wouldn't know a pretension if he stumbled over one, and the atmosphere of friendship at his Oak Supper Club near Pipestem reflects his philosophy that there are no strangers, only friends he hasn't met yet. His inn would be more appropriately named the White Oak Inn after the regal 800-year-old tree that stands in front of the converted nineteenth-century farmhouse. The magnificent tree, with its skyward reaching hydra of weighty limbs and Gibraltar-like trunk more than sixteen feet in circumference, is a fitting symbol of the steadfast quality of both the inn's food and the character of its owners.

"Good evening friends, welcome to the Oak," is Bollinger's standard greeting. The Bollingers live in the second floor of their inn and still view all who enter what used to be their own dining and living rooms as house guests. Although the interior is somewhat plain, it is homey.

The quality of the food combined with the friendliness probably make this the most enjoyable inn in West Virginia.

The chef is trained by Jim, and the style and types of food reflect both Jim's years as owner and manager of a large midwestern hotel and the earlier years he spent

ADDRESS: Pipestem, West Virginia 25979. It is one-half mile north of the Pipestem State Park Resort, off Route 20. Follow the well-marked signs with the oak tree emblem
TELEPHONE: 304-466-4800
FACILITIES: Dining only; April through October daily from 5 p.m. to midnight; closed Sundays and Mondays from November through March
RESERVATIONS: Recommended
DRESS: Casual
CREDIT CARDS: BankAmericard and Master Charge

as a wilderness canoe guide and cook in the northern reaches of Minnesota. Bollinger's country fare includes his own sourdough bread and smoked meats, and original soup, sauces, and salad dressings. The entrées include roast duckling, fresh trout, steaks, and barbecued ribs.

There are few things that Southerners get as chauvinistic about as the proper way to make barbecued ribs, and when the folk in this part of West Virginia heard that this fellow from Minnesota was trying to sell ribs, they were mighty skeptical. But the outcome of their skepticism is told in the fact that the ribs, prepared with Jim's own sauce, are the most popular dish with area natives, who are quick to confide that "you can't eat ribs proper without gettin' sauce under yer nails."

The sourdough chocolate cake is a unique end to a delicious meal, and a dessert that is rarely found anywhere in the east. It is difficult to choose among the desserts; one of the hardest choices for me was between the sourdough chocolate cake and the black walnut cake filled with sweet nutmeats.

Even the coffee is delicious. Try Jim's suggestion and drink a cup of tea with a slice of fresh lime squeezed in it. Dinner for two cost $22.

Bollinger and his wife raise championship Arabian horses, which occasionally can be seen in the nearby meadows and corrals.

CACAPON STATE PARK
BERKELEY SPRINGS, W. VA.

The day was warm for spring and we stepped slowly as we approached the summit of Cacapon Mountain. We had left the lodge about an hour and a half before and hiked one of the well-marked trails that thread their way through the more than 6,000 acres of Cacapon (pronounced "kah-kā-pon") State Park. The trees had just a green halo of new spring growth. Half an hour before, we had finished the brown bag lunches the lodge restaurant had packed for us. We had picked one of the relatively few flat spots along the trail and dined in the woods. The climb from the lodge would take us 1,400 feet to the top and back down again, along a five-mile circuit.

Hiking is only one of the many things, mostly outdoors, to do while staying at Cacapon. Evening marshmallow roasts and hayrides, nature programs presented by the park naturalist, golf, tennis, pedal boats, and fishing or sunning on the sand beach around the park's lake are only a few of the activities.

Cacapon Lodge is a stone and rough-wood structure with a restaurant and fifty guest rooms, all with private baths. The restaurant has the atmosphere of a grammar school cafeteria—checkered linoleum tile floors and Formica tables. The food, though adequate, is only a cut

ADDRESS: Route 522 about 10 miles south of Berkeley Springs, West Virginia 25411
TELEPHONE: 304-258-1022
FACILITIES: State park, lodge, and restaurant; Cacapon Lodge has a cafeteria and 50 guest rooms, the Old Inn has 11 rooms with shared baths, and cabins are available. Open year round, except some cabins; restaurant serves daily from 7:30 a.m. to 9 p.m.
RESERVATIONS: Required far in advance
RATES: $16.48 to $24.72
DRESS: Casual to blue jeans
CREDIT CARDS: BankAmericard and Master Charge

above your average roadside diner. The lodge often accepts large groups, which can be annoying. For that reason, the best stays in the park are in either the Old Inn, which has eleven rooms in a rough-hewn log structure, or in the rustic cabins, some of which are also made of logs. The Old Inn, with its wrought-iron fixtures, stone fireplace, and wide porch, is a delightful way to forget modern worries. The rooms are paneled in knotty pine and chestnut and have shared baths. The Old Inn is only open during the summer.

CANAAN VALLEY RESORT
DAVIS, W. VA.

The wind sweeps over the flatness of the Allegheny Plateau with such ferocity and tenacity that trees grow limbs only on their leeward sides. High above Canaan Valley (pronounced Ka-nane by the locals) the wilderness area of Dolly Sods remains for the hiker and backpacker to experience a climate that is so continually cold that it supports many alpine plants and animals.

This climate, with its heavy snowfall and cool summers, is the main attraction for those who visit the Canaan Valley Resort.

Located just off one of the few stretches of West Virginia Highway that can truly be called straight, Canaán Valley Resort was designed as a winter ski resort and boasts two chair lifts and a Poma lift to carry skiers to the top of its five open slopes and six trails. The lift base elevation is at 3,430 feet above sea level, the summit at 4,280 for a vertical drop of 850 feet.

But Canaan Valley Resort is open year round. It has a championship eighteen-hole golf course, nature trails, hiking trails, camping sites, and cabins, all within the park boundaries. Things here, though, are not big or impersonal, and though Canaan Valley is new, it keeps to the tradition of warm service for guests. The personnel

ADDRESS: Off Highway 32, about 8 miles south of Davis, West Virginia 26260. Take a right turn about two miles past the Canterbury Inn; drive slowly at night since the sign is unlighted and hard to see

TELEPHONE: 304-866-4121

FACILITIES: Main lodge, cabins for four, six, or eight persons fully equipped with electric heat, campsites with hookups. Restaurants in the ski lodge, the golf clubhouse, and the main lodge begin serving around 7:30 p.m. though hours vary with the seasons

RATES: Lodge: $24 for double. Cabins: 2 bedrooms are $42 first night and $22 each additional night

RESERVATIONS: A must for lodgings

DRESS: Casual in all restaurants and at all events; bring jeans and comfortable shoes

CREDIT CARDS: BankAmericard

at the golf pro shop or the ski shop are friendly and helpful. The restaurant staff are not that well trained, but with time and good management, the restaurant personnel—and its food—will no doubt improve.

There are three places to eat: the ski lodge, the golf clubhouse, and at the main lodge. The first two serve casual snack-bar foods, the last serves more substantial hot meals. The rooms in the lodge have typical motel décor, though, blessedly, none of them have television.

The four-, six-, or eight-person cabins are of a modern chalet-type construction. They're electrically heated and come fully equipped for housekeeping, including linens and kitchen utensils. They all have fireplaces and amply stocked woodsheds. Cabins must be rented for at least a full week in the summer.

The campground has sewer, electric and water hookups (except no water in the winter). The park has a naturalist in residence to conduct outdoor programs all year round, although the spring-summer-fall months are the most active. Activities include birdwalks, hikes to see beaver dams and habitats and to the National Forest Service's Dolly Sods Wilderness area, and special "listen to the sounds of night" hikes.

There is also an activities director to conduct special children's playtime and crafts activities, hayrides, hot dog roasts, movies, and to arrange white-water raft trips.

For campers, there is a country store that sells such staples as bread, beer, and blue jeans.

THE CANTERBURY INN
DAVIS, W. VA.

Historic buildings and centuries of service are not the only features that make a country inn. Occasionally someone manages to build a new inn from the ground up and fill it with the friendly spirit of the good old days.

The sunset had dropped below the ridges of the mountains and left Canaan Valley swimming in the warm afterglow of the evening when we arrived at the Canterbury Inn, about eight miles south of Davis and two miles north of the entrance to Canaan Valley State Park Resort. The warm natural wood tones of the Rocky Mountain modern architecture were a pleasing counterpoint to the grove of evergreens surrounding it.

Inside, the use of natural woods and stone made it at once secure and old, contemporary and inviting.

We were greeted by Joan Wright, who along with her husband, Joe, and silent partner, Charles McDonald, own the inn. They did much of the construction work themselves, but the apparent labor of love is the food. The Canterbury Inn is one of the few restaurants in the United States where cooking is done over live hardwood coals. The broiled beef dishes are without parallel; so are fish, shrimp, and chicken liver kabobs. Complete dinners include a well-stocked salad bar and bread

ADDRESS: Route 32, two miles north of the entrance to Canaan Valley State Park Resort, in Davis, West Virginia 26260
TELEPHONE: 304-866-4140
FACILITIES: Dining only; open year round, daily from 5 to 10:30 p.m.
RESERVATIONS: Required
DRESS: Nice casual to dressy, depending on your mood
CREDIT CARDS: American Express, BankAmericard, Master Charge, and personal checks

freshly baked and warm from the inn's ovens. Another unusual feature is a fine wine list that runs the gamut from a reasonably priced house wine to well-known American and vintage imported wines. Service is prompt, and best of all, a meal for two starting with French onion soup, followed by salad and two huge steaks (a tender filet mignon and a New York strip) accompanied by a bottle of wine, dessert, and coffee cost only $22.

Wide glass windows in the dining room allow you to enjoy the beauty of Canaan Valley—and the frequently appearing deer and other wildlife.

Joe Wright says that he is planning to eventually have overnight accommodations, but that is still several years away.

CHIMNEY CORNER DINING ROOM
RED HOUSE, MD.

There's something about a log cabin that just naturally says rustic. It conjures up images of Presidents, pancakes, syrups, and all that is good about rural America.

The Chimney Corner Dining Room in Red House is a log-cabin lodge with a cool front porch and well-tended window boxes brimming with red and white petunias. It was built in 1932 entirely out of the stone and timber that existed on the land then. Rather than the typical horizontal log construction, the solid chestnut logs of the Chimney Corner are arranged vertically in a stockade pattern, and the white mortar caulking provides a striped pattern. The windows and doors are trimmed with white birch branches, as are the solid chestnut tables inside.

The forty-by-eighty-foot building has open beam construction, which makes for cool breezy days in the summer; for winter there's a huge fireplace, built with thirty-five tons of stone.

Red House, Maryland (at the intersection of Routes 50 and 219), is only a mile or so from West Virginia, and belongs more to its panhandle than it does to Maryland. Route 50 runs almost entirely within West Virginia except for about five miles where cartographers looped

ADDRESS: At the intersection of Routes 50 and 219 in Red House, Maryland, a mile from the West Virginia border
TELEPHONE: 301-334-3040
FACILITIES: Dining only; daily from 9:30 a.m. to 8:30 p.m., hours sometimes shortened in winter
RESERVATIONS: Not accepted
DRESS: Casual
CREDIT CARDS: BankAmericard

the Maryland border south to snare Red House and confuse writers of inn books.

The Chimney Corner is built on the site of a former stagecoach stop located on the Northwestern Pike, which ran from Winchester, Virginia, to Parkersburg, West Virginia. The pike was completed in 1837 and travelers met at a red house here, which is how the crossroads got its name.

The food is as solid and un-fancy as the logs that hold up the roof. Country cooking featuring chicken and ham dominates the menu, but the real treat is breakfast. If you don't mind eating breakfast at noon or at suppertime, you can enjoy raised buckwheat pancakes and real maple syrup. Those who have never had honest-to-goodness buckwheat cakes will find the flavor stronger than in the bleached flour monstrosities civilization forces upon us. A side order of sausage is a lean and meaty delight. Dinner for two cost $10.

When you pay your bill, be sure to pay your respects to Teddy Roosevelt, whose picture stares out from behind the counter. It seems that when owner Bill Smith's grandfather was a local sheriff at the turn of the century, he received the picture as a reward for his work on behalf of the Rough Rider. The picture was passed on to Bill's father, who bought the Chimney Corner in 1935 and who couldn't think of a better person to look after the cash register.

COOLFONT
BERKELEY SPRINGS, W. VA.

Brahms by the brook, country in the kitchen, trekking on the horse trails, fun by the bushel. If it can be done outdoors, crafted indoors, sung or picked on a banjo, eaten, drunk, or enjoyed, you can't do it at a better place than the Coolfont vacation center just outside Berkeley Springs, West Virginia.

Coolfont offers campsites, good dining, rental cabins and chalets, water sports, crafts, and music. And if you like it enough to stay a long while, you can buy your own lot and build a chalet.

The Treetop House restaurant serves some of the best broiled rainbow trout that can be eaten. Its incredibly sweet taste is due in no small part to the fact that the fish is just hours from the fishing hole. Veal Marsala, fresh crab cakes, and other seafood in season are equally well prepared. The gargantuan salad bar often has as many as twenty-seven fresh vegetables, and the accompanying bread bar offers rye, Italian, French, and pumpernickel. The wildflower mountain honey is locally produced and has a taste that can't be matched. Dinner for two cost $24.

The restaurant is located in a natural wood and stone lodge that looks like a Rocky Mountain chalet. Also in the lodge is the Squirrels Nest, an informal lounge

ADDRESS: Cold Run Valley Road, Berkeley Springs, West Virginia 25411. Drive south on Route 522 about 4 miles from Berkeley Springs (or 3.5 miles north of the Cacapon State Park entrance); turn west at the Treetop sign. Coolfont is three miles from the turnoff

TELEPHONE: 304-258-1793

FACILITIES: Lodging and dining; rental chalets ranging from 3 bedrooms for 9 people to log cabins for 1 to 4 people; bunk-like dormitory accommodations also available. Lunch Monday through Saturday from 11:30 a.m. to 2 p.m. and from 2 p.m. to 5 p.m. for cold sandwiches only. Dinner served Monday through Thursday from 5 to 9 p.m., Fridays and Saturdays until 10 p.m., Sundays noon to 8:30 p.m.

RATES: Three-bedroom chalets from $220 to $265 per week, rustic log cabins from $110 to $120 per week. During the summer, rentals are limited to one-week minimums

RESERVATIONS: Required

DRESS: Nice casual

CREDIT CARDS: None

with live musical entertainment on weekends. The music runs to bluegrass and Appalachian mountain music, but the Coolfont artists-in-residence program has included such classical groups as the Reston string quartet.

Many of the rental chalets are privately owned units, rented by the Coolfont management. They range from three-bedroom chalets with room for nine people to rustic log cabins for one to four people. Bunk-like accommodations are also available. During the summer, rentals are limited to one-week minimums, although the management welcomes weekend stays during other seasons.

Coolfont offers the standard recreational fare — golfing, tennis, swimming—but it also has a variety of guided nature walks, crafts programs for children and adults, guided trail rides, and the benefits of the artists and musicians in residence. The strawberry festival in May is a delightful mélange of craftspeople, flea marketeers, hootenanny singers, musicians, and families who've come to enjoy them all. On this and several other holiday weekends rental rates increase 25 percent.

Coolfont's 1,800-acre site at the foot of Cacapon Mountain is complete with lake and beach, a dock for diving, and plenty of space for sun worshippers. No fishing license is necessary for the lake and streams, and an extra fishing pole is available for those who forget theirs.

COUNTRY INN
BERKELEY SPRINGS, W. VA.

I t's hard to think of our Revolutionary forefathers actually having fun, what with throwing off the yoke of colonialism and with the hardships inflicted by red-coated British and Hessian mercenaries.

But when our first President wanted a vacation, he headed back to a spot he had discovered while surveying the wilderness for Lord Fairfax—Berkeley Springs, West Virginia. Of course, when George Washington was President, there was no West Virginia and no town called Berkeley Springs. What there was, was a mineral spring that native Americans and our number one President thought had curative and restorative powers.

Washington discovered the springs in 1748 and built a summer home nearby in 1784. Other people built there too, including three signers of the Declaration of Independence, Charles Carroll, James Smith, and James Wilson; a bevy of Revolutionary generals; and six members of the Continental Congress. Washington's summer White House was destroyed by fire in 1870, but the homes of many other prominent people in history still stand, though most are not open to the public.

The springs were an attraction in colonial times, and in 1776, the Town of Bath was formed. According to the legislative decree, fifty acres were set aside for

ADDRESS: Route 522 in Berkeley Springs, West Virginia 25411. The inn will provide transportation to and from Hancock, Maryland (6 miles away), for guests arriving by Amtrak, but arrangements for this service must be made in advance
TELEPHONE: 304-258-2210
FACILITIES: 37 rooms; breakfast from 7 to 10 a.m., lunch from 11:45 a.m. to 2 p.m., dinner from 5:30 to 8:30 p.m. except Sundays when dinner is served from noon to 7 p.m. Open year round
RATES: $14 for a single with shared bath, $27 for a double with a master bedroom, $37 for four people
RESERVATIONS: Required
DRESS: Nice casual in the dining room
CREDIT CARDS: American Express, BankAmericard, and Master Charge

the town and one spring was reserved for use by the "poor and infirm people and suffering humanity." This act reserving an area for public use produced the first state park in the nation.

This park, complete with springs and bathhouse, now sits only yards from the Country Inn, which was built in 1932. Its colonial brick structure and imposing white columns make it a landmark in Berkeley Springs. The inn is a friendly place. The public rooms have the atmosphere of a private living room, with mementos scattered among a curious mixture of end tables, corner shelves, overstuffed chairs, and sofas. The game room is furnished with refugees of a rummage sale. Odd moments browsing among the old books and furnishings will provide no small amount of amusement to those born in the past three decades. All the furnishings are comfortable; there's something secure about a décor that is not larger than life and intimidating. There's very little here that looks like a hotel.

The inn does well with a modest but enjoyable menu of country cooking. Ham, chicken, beef, and seafood are well prepared and served in a high-ceilinged dining room with wood paneling. Winter meals are a delight taken in the glow of flames from the fireplace. Dinner for two cost $17.

A family-like atmosphere prevails, and you may be followed to your room by a fluffy, gray, long-haired house cat that calls the inn its own, or you may be asked to lock up and turn out the lights if you are planning to stay out late.

George Washington's baths are still operating next door to the Country Inn, but are under the control of the State of West Virginia. This is the no-frills version of what you might find at some privately run mineral water spas, but for $7 you get a massage and choice of Roman, steam baths, or heat treatments.

Special packages are available through the Country Inn, so check ahead. A typical winter package—costing less than $70—brought the following for two people: two nights' lodging, two dinners, two breakfasts, two mineral baths and massages, and two cocktails in the small lounge.

Golf, tennis, horseback riding, hiking, hunting, and fishing are all available nearby.

FORT SAVANNAH INN
LEWISBURG, W. VA.

Early settlers used to wage desperate battles for survival here against native Americans who resented the colonial intrusion and fought to keep their land. The present-day Fort Savannah Inn is located on the original site of Fort Savannah, which later grew into the town of Lewisburg. The owners of the inn are in the process of recreating a complete and architecturally accurate replica of the original fort. One main building—now used as the dining room—a couple of outbuildings, and a museum have been completed, and other buildings are in the planning stages.

Lewisburg was named after Fort Savannah's commander, General Andrew Lewis, who commanded the troops in the opening battle of the American Revolution at Point Pleasant in 1774.

Other historical attractions nearby include the Old Stone Church, which has been in continuous use since 1796, a Confederate cemetery, and the Lost World Caverns. Also nearby is the General Lewis Inn, which dates from 1798.

As we walked into the Fort Savannah Inn, we were confronted by a huge antique loom, with a rainbow of warp and weft. The cavernous interior of the inn, with its high-pitched ceiling and open beams, really did give

ADDRESS: 204 North Jefferson Street, Lewisburg, West Virginia 24901. It is a block-and-a-half north of Route 60 on Route 219
TELEPHONE: 304-645-3055
FACILITIES: 40 rooms. Dining daily from 6 a.m. to 9 p.m.
RATES: $18 for double
RESERVATIONS: Not necessary for dining, but recommended for overnight accommodations
DRESS: Casual
CREDIT CARDS: American Express, BankAmericard, Carte Blanche, Master Charge

us the feeling of walking into an old fort blockhouse. The fare was plain small-town-café cooking, with sandwiches as the lunch specialities and country standards—chicken, beef, and ham—for dinner. The meal was good and inexpensive; we paid $6 for two for lunch, which included a huge, homemade apple dumpling with ice cream.

The lodgings that the inn offers in a separate building are strictly commercial hotel; they are clean and well kept but have no special charm.

The Fort Savannah is the ideal place to lunch for those staying at the General Lewis Inn, which only serves breakfast and evening dinner.

GENERAL LEWIS INN
LEWISBURG, W. VA.

Every nook and cranny of the General Lewis Inn in Lewisburg is filled with some sort of antique, collectible, or memorabile. Although the main part of the inn dates from 1798, the focus of its collection is on the Civil War era.

The majestic colonial-columned structure has many additions added over a century and a half by various owners, and a commanding hilltop position. Its green lawn flows past the crescent driveway down to Washington Street, the main street of Lewisburg. An antique auto, protected by its own diminutive gazebo, rests on the front lawn, as if its owner had just parked it there while taking a meal at the inn. Inside, the cozy dining room with its memento-laden stone fireplace and wooden floors gives you a good indication of the treasures found throughout the rest of the inn—every room is filled with antiques.

All of the guest rooms are furnished with antiques, poster beds, brass beds, candle stands, and patchwork quilts. The rooms, for the most part, are small and cramped, but it's hard to mind lack of space that is caused primarily by the presence of so many beautiful pieces of furniture.

Memory Hall, at the rear of the lobby, is filled with

ADDRESS: 301 E. Washington Street, Lewisburg, West Virginia 24901

TELEPHONE: 304-645-2600

FACILITIES: 30 rooms with TV, most with private bath. Breakfast daily from 7 to 9:30 a.m., dinner from 5:30 to 8 p.m. Noon meal served on Sundays only

RATES: $11 to $17

RESERVATIONS: Recommended for both rooms and meals

DRESS: Nice casual to informal

CREDIT CARDS: American Express

Civil War newspapers, uniforms, and flags, which give insight into the problems that troubled the republic more than 100 years ago.

If you arrive in the spring or summer the rock and flower gardens in the rear are beautiful, and there are benches throughout on which to read, daydream, or admire the scenery.

A Civil War history marker sits at the roadside in front of the inn and tells the bemused reader that in 1862 Confederate troops "were repulsed" by a Union force.

But there is no way that anyone could "be repulsed" by the General Lewis Inn's food. The dining room specializes in country favorites: pork chops, ham, fried chicken, and steak. The food is good and the service is cheery.

HILLTOP HOUSE
HARPERS FERRY, W. VA.

The twin river gorges where the Potomac and the Shenandoah Rivers mix is an inspiring sight that is less likely to provoke stark wonderment than quiet revery. The sight has always fascinated Americans and no doubt was a favorite place for native Americans when it belonged to them. But one of its biggest lovers was Thomas Jefferson. In fact, a good spot to contemplate the beauty is from a site called Jefferson Rock, reached by steps from the restored federal town, the Harpers Ferry National Park. Jefferson is thought to have said of the sight that it was "worth a trip across the Atlantic to see."

We found it beautiful but not perhaps worth a trip across the Atlantic. You'll find very good views after arduous hikes to the top of the Maryland Heights Cliffs, and from the cliffs in Virginia around Chimney Rock just off the Appalachian trail (maps for the Maryland Heights trail are available at the National Park information office in Harpers Ferry).

One of the nicest vantage points is from the Hilltop House, a fifty-five-room inn that rests at the top of a sheer cliff overlooking the town of Harpers Ferry and the rivers' confluence.

The inn was once a favorite retreat for famous

ADDRESS: Just off High Street in Harpers Ferry, West Virginia 25425. Signs along High Street point the way
TELEPHONE: 304-535-6321
FACILITIES: 55 rooms; dining from 7:30 to 10 a.m. and noon to 8 p.m.
RATES: $10 to $11 for a single, $19 to $22 for a double
RESERVATIONS: Required for rooms; not required for meals, but you may want to check ahead to see whether a large group is expected
DRESS: Casual
CREDIT CARDS: None

Americans—Woodrow Wilson and Mark Twain to name two—and today is popular for bus tours and carloads of families. What was a sleepy inn suitable for reflection and contemplation is now a bustling center of activity, especially on summer weekends, with arts and crafts shows, flower shows, Easter egg hunts, and old-time silent films. The lobby is usually a manic mixture of hotel guests, day visitors, and members of group tours visiting the gift shop, looking at the special displays, or trying to get into the dining room.

The dining room has several sections, some of which are better than others if you want to do your sightseeing while you eat. The rooms on the end of the inn are best for scenery. The food is plentiful, and the weekends feature a buffet lunch, all you can eat. We wished that there were more incentive to go back for seconds; although the food is adequately prepared, it is bland and uninspiring. The individually ordered dinners available when the buffet is not offered are much better, but overpriced at $4.50 to $5.95. The menu runs to steaks and chicken and some pre-prepared seafood dishes.

Hilltop House was built in the late 1890's and later purchased and renovated by D. C. Kilham, a Baltimore attorney. All of the rooms have air conditioning and many have private baths, but despite this they are not very comfortable.

IRON HORSE INN
HARPERS FERRY, W. VA.

The hot July sun had taken its toll, and the sights of the restored federal town of Harpers Ferry were now taking second place to our search for a glass of something cold to drink and a place to sit and lunch.

After passing a couple of fast-food hamburger and frozen custard shops, whose plastic and paper utensils had become litter decorating the cobblestones, we began to despair. Then we drew near the train station. First we came to the toy train museum—an old boxcar stuffed full of things to drive a railroad buff crazy and strike little kids with awe. Then we saw the Iron Horse Inn.

The inn is on Potomac Street and is unchallenged for the best food in town. The federal armory, which made Harpers Ferry a vital target in the Civil War and formed the basis of the town's industry, was also on Potomac Street. In fact, the building in which the Iron Horse Inn is located was once the armory superintendent's home and is one of the few armory buildings that has survived the brutal punishment of the long succession of floods that carried away buildings, people, and the town's industrial vitality.

The armory superintendent's former home, though, has been preserved and the folks who now occupy it serve

ADDRESS: Potomac Street, Harpers Ferry, West Virginia 25425
TELEPHONE: 304-535-6617
FACILITIES: Dining only; Monday through Friday from 11 a.m. to 6 p.m., until 7:30 p.m. on weekends and on some holidays when they serve buffet style. Winter hours may vary so you might want to call ahead
RESERVATIONS: None
DRESS: Neat casual
CREDIT CARDS: None

a mean ham sandwich, stacked thick with thin-sliced cured ham. Country fried chicken and steaks are among the most popular items on the menu. Although their cooking is plain and the menu limited, what is served is food that most restaurants are too lazy to prepare. The fresh-baked apple pie is just that—freshly baked and full of real apples, with none of the gummy paste that some call crust and no chemicals and dried apple bits.

Besides the quality of the food and the friendliness of the people, the best thing about this inn is a tariff so low that you'd swear somebody added up the check wrong. On the afternoon we ate there the bill for stuffing three people came to under six dollars.

MOUNTAIN CREEK LODGE
PIPESTEM, W. VA.

Finding the footprints of deer and fox at your doorstep, falling asleep to the mountain breezes, and rising to gaze at the ghostly shapes of trees in the early morning fog are West Virginia experiences that make you believe in the wonderful of the state's "wild, wonderful West Virginia" slogan.

Set in the middle of this splendor, and built so that it blends rather than fights with its surroundings, is the Mountain Creek Lodge, a smaller and more remote section of the Pipestem Resort. The Mountain Creek Lodge sits at the bottom of the Bluestone River Gorge, close enough to go to sleep each night to the rustle of the river over its rounded rocks and boulders. The lodge achieves intimacy and separation from the main resort by being accessible only by a cable tram that transports visitors from the edge of the Bluestone River gorge to the lodge, which is at the bottom of the tree-lined canyon. Although the lodge is a new building, it is small and cozy, and has a lovely lobby with a fireplace.

Hiking, fishing, wading in the river, or browsing through the tiny bookshop by the restaurant are the favorite activities. The little bookshop specializes in West Virginia memorabilia and history, and possesses an amazing collection of first editions, rare books, and other

ADDRESS: Pipestem State Park Resort, Pipestem, West Virginia 25979. It is three miles off Route 20, halfway between Princeton and Hinton
TELEPHONE: 304-466-1800
FACILITIES: 30 rooms in Mountain Creek Lodge, 113 rooms in main lodge, 25 cottages, campsites for tents and motor homes. Mountain Creek Lodge open June to September; main lodge open year round. Dining from 7 a.m. to 9 p.m., available in Mountain Creek Dining Room, a snack bar, cafeteria, or cafe, all within the park
RATES: Single rooms $12-$18 in main lodge, $14-$16 in Mountain Creek Lodge. Weekly cottage rental $152-$195 for two-bedroom; three and four bedroom cottages available at higher prices
RESERVATIONS: Recommended
DRESS: Nice casual to informal in Mountain Creek Dining Room; anything you want to wear elsewhere in resort
CREDIT CARDS: BankAmericard and Master Charge

hard-to-find reading material. Fishing lures, flashlights for midnight skulking, insect repellent, and other items of use in the canyon are also available here.

The dining room at the Mountain Creek Lodge serves dishes like shrimp scampi, *coq au vin,* and broiled lobster tails. The meals, which began with French onion soup and ended with Mountain High Pie, will not soon be forgotten.

Our room in the lodge had a spectacular view of the canyon—very early one morning I awoke to the breathtaking sight of fog settling in the gorge.

The main lodge at Pipestem offers its own, though not as intimate, diversions and recreation. The imposing wood and stone structure perches at the edge of the gorge and also has beautiful views of sunsets and scenery. There is a championship golf course, a par three course, and a miniature golf course, as well as tennis courts that are located next to the main lodge. Ice skating in the winter, a health club with saunas, an indoor and an outdoor swimming pool, horseback riding, folk crafts, performing musicians, an outdoor amphitheater with Sunday church services and weekend musical entertainment are all part of the attractions here.

The resort also offers cottages complete with fireplaces and wood supplies, and there is a campground with fifty sites for both tents and motor homes.

Pipestem has 4,000 acres of its own and is surrounded by a 25,000-acre game management area. This section of West Virginia is so sparsely populated that the area around Pipestem is almost entirely composed of trees, mountains, and fresh air, with little sign of human life.

At Hinton, fourteen miles from Pipestem, the Bluestone, Greenbrier, and New rivers merge. The New River is the oldest river in the western hemisphere. Depending on water conditions, raft trips are available on all of the rivers, but check with the front desk at the main lodge to confirm dates and places.

MOUNTAIN VILLAGE INN
DAVIS, W. VA.

A summer thundershower had left Silver Lake with figures of mist strolling over the water. Bright green leaves were accented by the moisture. Outside the window of the Mountain Village Inn in Davis, light that filtered over the evergreens framing the lake grew fainter. Suddenly, like giant bumblebees, first one, then a pair, finally a trio of hummingbirds hovered over the rhododendron that bloomed just outside.

Moments before we had threaded a careful path through the rain on the switchbacks of the West Virginia mountains—it seemed more like being in the Bavarian alps than in the good old United States. The Mountain Village Inn completed the image by looking like a chalet in the Black Forest, with rough-sawn, board-and-batten siding and gingerbread decoration.

Alpine chalets are almost synonymous with cheery service and good food, and we weren't disappointed. In the pine-paneled dining room, we found homemade bread, steaks brought sizzling to the table, great seafood, country ham, and a modest but satisfying salad bar. The homemade cakes, especially the cherry chip cake, are confectionary treasures, worth every calorie of the diet that must be broken to enjoy them. Full meals for two

ADDRESS: Route 219 ten miles north of Davis, West Virginia 26260
TELEPHONE: 304-735-6344
FACILITIES: Dining only; Monday through Saturday from 5 to 9 p.m., Sunday 1 to 9 p.m.
RESERVATIONS: Accepted but not always necessary
DRESS: Casual
CREDIT CARDS: None

with dessert and including wine cost $11.52.

There are seats available on the porch outside, but they get wet when it rains. If you don't mind the insects and want to sit and listen to the sounds of the evening, though, the porch is a perfect place.

There's horseback riding nearby, and boats and fishing gear can be rented for modest prices at the lake.

Across the road is what claims to be the smallest church in the United States. This quaint, diminutive structure was built by Lithuanian immigrants, Mr. and Mrs. Peter L. Milknit, who came to America in 1893.

SCOLLAY HALL
MIDDLEWAY, W. VA.

The porch sags a bit, and the windows need some paint, but the antique brick structure has grown old gracefully, nestled among and cooled by the massive maple trees that have grown old along with it. It's been a while since anything changed around the Scollay Hall Dining Room and maybe that's just the way Mrs. Louise Smith Bradley wants it. After all, her ancestor John Smith founded the little town of Middleway back in 1729—she has the original papers and plat of the town ready for the curious eye. Middleway is not much larger now than when Smith founded it and though it was once prosperous—it had five inns—it slowly declined after being bypassed by the railroads.

One thing that has not declined with passing years is the quality of the food at Scollay Hall. The corn soufflé, the homemade rolls, and the chocolate cake are all delicious. The entrée selection is limited, which enables Mrs. Bradley to put more time into the house specialties: crab imperial, country ham, and southern fried chicken. Dinner for two cost $16. Even though Mrs. Bradley often has trouble getting qualified employees and has to do all the work herself (she is in her seventies), her standards are as high as those of any grandmother who ever made Christmas dinner for her family.

ADDRESS: Middleway, West Virginia 25430. Drive seven miles north of Charlestown on Route 51 until you come to a gasoline station at the corner of Route 48. Turn left here; Middleway is only a few hundred yards down the road. Scollay Hall will be on the left. Parking is available in the field on the right side of the road
TELEPHONE: 304-725-7428
FACILITIES: Dining only; Monday through Friday from 4 to 8 p.m., Saturdays from noon to 8 p.m.
RESERVATIONS: Necessary, preferably a day ahead
DRESS: Nice casual to informal
CREDIT CARDS: None

We arrived one Saturday afternoon just as Mrs. Bradley had arrived at the inn with her Saturday shopping, fresh for that day's meals. She showed us around the house, built in 1789 and named after a medical school classmate who later joined John Smith to practice medicine in what was then called Smithfield (later changed when the town of ham fame became so well known). Because of the number of doctors—there were seven here at one time—Middleway was neutral ground in the Civil War as the wounded and injured from both sides were taken here for treatment.

The house has beautiful carved walnut doors, molding, and an enormous hand-carved staircase rail. But more fascinating than the antique architecture is the legend of the demon that once inhabited the small hamlet. The legend of Wizard Clip tells of a bigoted Protestant in the mid-1700s who was confronted with a sick visitor one stormy night. He took the visitor in and put him to bed, shortly after which the man, who was Catholic, realized he was dying and asked for a priest. The home's owner refused to travel the eight miles in the storm to bring in a Popish visitor, and so the man died without proper rites and was given a Protestant burial. Shortly afterwards, the man's cattle died and mysterious noises plagued his house. Weirdest were invisible scissors that cut strange half moons or crescents in the linens, sheets, blankets, and clothes. Finally one day the victim had a vision—he was directed to get a priest to consecrate the dead visitor's grave. When this was done, the clipping stopped, and the grateful man gave the Catholic church forty acres of land along Opequon Creek. A chapel has been built on the land and church meetings are held there.

TIDEWATER VIRGINIA

The story of the Tidewater area of Virginia is the story of colonial America. The first permanent English settlement was here at Jamestown, as was the colonial capital of Williamsburg.

Williamsburg still remains as the biggest attraction of this region, and the quality with which the old capitol and picturesque town have been restored makes all of the attention directed toward it well deserved.

Nearby is the site at Yorktown, where the colonials won an important victory in 1781, and the restored site of Jamestown.

Richmond, which served as the capital of the United States

in 1780 and as the capital of the Confederacy eighty years later, is not far away. Today, there are still many Civil War reminders within the city and in the surrounding countryside.

Also worth visiting in Richmond, especially for fans of suspense and terror, is the Edgar Allen Poe Museum, filled with exhibits from this famous writer's life. For some modern-day entertainment, there are two theme parks à la Disneyland in the area—Kings Dominion north of Richmond, and Busch Gardens adjacent to Williamsburg.

Throughout the region, especially along the James and Potomac Rivers, beautifully restored plantations capture the feeling of a bygone era. Moving northeast from Richmond, across that part of Virginia known as the Northern Neck, is Stratford Hall, the most unique of all Virginia plantations. This was the birthplace of the Lee family, which gave us two signers of the Declaration of Independence, Revolutionary War heroes, and the commander of the Army of the Confederacy. Just up the road, but not as well restored or as elaborate as the Lee home, are the birthplaces of George Washington and James Madison.

Colonial Williamsburg Photograph

CHRISTIANA CAMPBELL'S TAVERN
WILLIAMSBURG, VA.

There are three restored taverns in historic Williamsburg that now serve food to the public: Josiah Chowning's Tavern and The King's Arms Tavern, both on Duke of Gloucester Street, and Christiana Campbell's Tavern on Waller Street. All three buildings are restored in the letter-perfect fashion in which everything is done in Williamsburg, but admire The King's Arms and Chowning's Tavern from the outside. Only Christiana Campbell's has food and service that is worth waiting for. It's hard to figure out why the wide disparity in cooking exists, since all three inns are operated by the Colonial Williamsburg Foundation.

Christiana Campbell's Tavern is furnished with original eighteenth-century antiques and reproductions, and is decorated in the simple fashion that was typical of the last half of the 1700's. American and English Windsor chairs and ladder back chairs sit before a variety of tables. The corner cupboards, serving table, and dresser are authentic antiques, as are the maps, decorative pewter, and much of the ceramics. The tableware pattern is taken from a design made in mid-eighteenth-century England.

Christiana Campbell's is on Waller Street at the extreme east end of Duke of Gloucester Street, somewhat

ADDRESS: Waller Street, Williamsburg, Virginia 23185
TELEPHONE: 804-229-2141
FACILITIES: Dining only; open for lunch from 11:30 a.m. to 3 p.m., dinner beginning at 5:30 p.m.
RESERVATIONS: Required for dinner, not accepted for lunch
DRESS: Casual
CREDIT CARDS: None

hidden behind the old capitol. The two-storied building has an inviting front porch and a gambrel roof. It was in use as a tavern by 1765, though no one is certain exactly when it was built. Then, as today, the tavern enjoyed a reputation for being a cut above its competition. A French traveler remarked that it was "where all the best people resorted." It was a favorite of the Virginia colony legislators, who met across the street from the tavern when Williamsburg was the capital. In 1772, a year after Mrs. Campbell took over the operation of the tavern, George Washington recorded in his diary that he ate here often during his attendance at the House of Burgesses.

Dining is available both inside the tavern and in a small garden in the rear when the weather permits. The food is delicious and reasonably priced. A chicken pot pie was thick with chicken and vegetables and was well seasoned. The meat-filled pastries were also hearty and delicious. And we were in heaven with the warm apple turnovers and the rum cream pie with chocolate shavings. A complete meal for two people cost less than $10.

Lovely overnight accommodations are available in several of the restored homes in Historic Williamsburg. The Williamsburg Inn's guest houses are particularly nice. However, reservations must be made far in advance by contacting the Colonial Williamsburg Foundation, Williamsburg, Virginia 23185.

THE EAGLE'S NEST
KILMARNOCK, VA.

"These pins here are made of locust wood," said Wes Jones, as he rapped one against the table and listened to it hum like a metal bar. "I got them from an old shipyard. Shipbuilders used them to put their boats together with. I used them to put my tavern together with," he said pointing to the rows of trimmed pegs that fastened the massive wooden beams.

The Eagle's Nest Tavern, just north of Kilmarnock on Route 3, is a replica of an eighteenth-century tidewater Virginia ordinary. Jones and his friends built it from the ground up, entirely out of old materials. The beams came from an old Confederate warehouse in Richmond that had been torn down, the bricks from the foundation of an old building that had burned. Jones said that he faithfully copied the plans from records available in the courthouse in New Kent.

The interior successfully captures the feel of the old tavern: rough adz-marked beams, a massive mantel crowning a fireplace of handmade bricks and covered with antiques and reproductions, simple pine tables and ladder back chairs, and worn random-width flooring, the surface of which has been sanded and shaped by more than a century of sole-scuffing, though not all of it at this location.

ADDRESS: Route 3, Kilmarnock, Virginia 22482
TELEPHONE: 804-435-3661
FACILITIES: Dining only; open Labor Day until May, Monday through Friday from 5 p.m. to 1 a.m., Saturday and Sunday from noon to 1 a.m.; during the summer open daily from noon to 1 a.m.
RESERVATIONS: Not required, but appreciated
DRESS: Casual
CREDIT CARDS: BankAmericard and Master Charge

The food, too, matches the mood. No fancy sauces or elaborate dishes here—you'd hardly have expected complicated fare had you stumbled out of a cold night into a place like this 200 years ago. The menu runs heavily to seafood, sandwiches, and salads.

We tried the shrimp salad, a huge collection of shrimp blended with celery and their own sauce. And the dish of beef barbecue was the best I have eaten since the last time I ate at Leonards, a place in Memphis that is generally acknowledged to have the best barbecue in the South. (Not barbecued ribs, but the meaty chunks of barbecue that come from roasting an entire side of beef or pork for hours in a pit of hickory coals.) Leonard's has a guarantee that if you can find barbecue anywhere that is better than theirs, they'll buy you a meal; I'm not quite ready to apply for that free meal, but came very close after eating barbecue at the Eagle's Nest.

To top the meal off, the homemade pecan pie was served hot.

There are no overnight accommodations at Eagle's Nest, but it is an ideal spot for lunch if you are staying at the Tides Lodge in Irvington and are driving around to see the quaint Chesapeake Bay fishing villages — Reedsville and Windmill Point are two that are very quaint and interesting.

FOX HEAD INN
MANAKIN, VA.

An evening at the Fox Head Inn near Manakin, Virginia, is a giant step backward in time to a period when graciousness was a way of life. The inn is a huge white country home with a circular drive that arcs its way from the main road, through a brace of tall oaks, past the front door, and then back to the road. The hills and fields along the main road are lined with the sleek thoroughbreds contained by the white wooden fences that are so typical of horse country. And this is horse country, deep in the fox hunting territory of Goochland County. The Deep Run Hunt Club is just a stone's throw from the inn.

The massive inn was built around the turn of this century and has been restored to reflect the flavor of that period. Antiques throughout the inn make a visit here as delightful for examining the furnishing as it is for dining.

Each of the four intimate dining rooms—The Country Kitchen, The Tobacco Room, The Hunt Room, and the Thoroughbred Room—has its own theme. The Country Kitchen is decorated with a collection of old skillets, pots, pans, and other kitchen ware, and a collection of rare blue granite ware, all hung on the soft weathered grey barn boards that once paneled the exterior of a barn.

ADDRESS: Manakin, Virginia 23103. Take I-64 to the Manakin-Route 623 Exit south. Go 1¼ miles to Route 250; turn right. Go 1 mile to intersection with Route 621 and turn left; the inn is on the right about a mile down the road
TELEPHONE: 804-784-5126
FACILITIES: Dining only; open Monday through Saturday at 6:30 p.m.
RESERVATIONS: Required days in advance
DRESS: Informal
CREDIT CARDS: None

The Tobacco Room is filled with memorabilia of the filthy weed, complete with an old Bull Durham poster like the ones once seen on the sides of barns through the countryside and an old wooden cigar-store Indian.

We ate in the Hunt Room, which is decorated in the pinks of the fox hunter's garb. This is idyllic in the winter, when a fire is working in the hearth. The hunting and coach horns, an English tapestry, and other decorations in this room make one feel rather regal and ready for the hounds.

Another ''shoe-in'' for good dining is the Thoroughbred Room, filled with the pictures of winning horses from local stables, the colors of local jockeys, and saddles from Europe.

The most astounding thing is that the food measures up to the setting. So many times we've visited inns where the magnificent surroundings completely overshadow rather weak cuisine and service. Not here.

Homemade salad dressings on fresh greens and vegetables; Sally Lunn bread hot from the oven; a seafood casserole packed with shrimp, lobster, crab, and scallops in a delicate Newburg sauce; and prime ribs thick, tender, done to the perfect degree of pinkness. This was all topped off by fox hunter's pie, a memorable chocolate-pecan pie that is far more worth pursuing than a fox. A meal for two cost about $24.

The meal selection process is unabashedly sexist: women get menus without any prices. Another unusual feature of the inn is its upstairs sitting rooms. The Fox Head Inn takes reservations for sittings, and under this system guests arrive about forty-five minutes before they are seated at a table and occupy the sitting rooms. This is a great place to come with a party of four to eight people, since you can converse with your friends in a setting not unlike your own living room (each sitting room can comfortably accommodate about eight people).

In these rooms you are the guests of Phillip and Barbara Pettit, the owners of the inn, who also live here. You can use their mixers and ice and glasses to prepare drinks from the liquor you brought yourself. BYOB? Yep, Goochland County is dry. But in these rooms you're the guest of the owners, and there is no charge for any of the mixers or for the crackers and dip.

HALFWAY HOUSE
RICHMOND, VA.

In the middle of one of the most garish spots of Route 1, amid the McDonald's and a myriad of imitators, is the Halfway House, an oasis for the eye and for the stomach. It is as welcome today as it was 200 years ago when it was the only place to eat, a stagecoach stop halfway between Richmond and Petersburg.

The house was built in 1760 on land granted by King George II, and the list of famous personalities who enjoyed the inn's hospitality reads like a high-school history book. According to Fred and Jay Bender, the inn's owners, George Washington, Marquis de Lafayette, Patrick Henry, Thomas Jefferson, Robert E. Lee, Ulysses S. Grant, and James Whitcomb Riley were only a few of the inn's illustrious visitors.

The Halfway House served as the headquarters of the Union's General Butler during the siege of Richmond, until his troops were defeated by Lee in 1864.

The interior of the dining room looks today much, I imagine, as it looked at the time of Butler's withdrawal. Diners enter the dining room, which is in the basement, through a screen door under the rear porch and to one side of the back steps. The low ceiling and dark walls give it a conspiratorial air.

The best advice a diner here can take is to skip all

ADDRESS: 10301 Jefferson Davis Highway, Richmond, Virginia 23234. Take I-95 to Exit 6A and go on Route 1/301 south for 1½ miles. Or take Exit 6 to Route 1/301 and go north 1½ miles

TELEPHONE: 804-275-1760

FACILITIES: Dining only; Monday through Saturday from 5:30 to 11 p.m., Sundays from 4:30 to 11 p.m.

RESERVATIONS: Required

DRESS: Nice casual to informal

CREDIT CARDS: American Express, BankAmericard, Carte Blanche, Diner's Club, Master Charge

the openers and go straight to the main courses. We started out with a sparkling Burgundy cocktail that didn't sparkle (it was replaced by one that did after quite a wait), onion soup with soggy bread croutons and a dish of half stale grated cheese to put on top, and a mediocre salad.

But the entrées were good enough to make up for the previous courses' shortcomings and left us feeling that we would not hesitate to eat here again. The fried shrimp were fresh, not greasy. Shan's chicken liver and onions were prepared with the same light batter as the shrimp and were very good.

The entrée was accompanied by fresh carrots and southern-style green beans prepared with ham. Homemade rolls and cinnamon muffins were served hot from the oven. Desserts were nothing sensational; I'd rather skip dessert and have seconds on the cinnamon buns. Dinner for two cost $29.

HANOVER TAVERN
HANOVER, VA.

Patrick Henry may have regretted that he had but one life to give for his country, but it's certain that he had no regrets about the life he injected into the Hanover Tavern. Legend has it that he was quite accomplished at fiddling, and between sets with his fiddle and stands at denouncing the king, it seems that he did a bit of fiddling around with the tavern owner's daughter, Sarah Shelton. Before he knew it, he was married to her and drawing ale as the Hanover Tavern's barkeep. I can just hear old innkeeper Shelton grumbling about not being able to get good help anymore on the day when Patrick had to walk across the street to the Hanover Courthouse and deliver his first famous public oration, known as the "Parson's Cause."

Founded as a stagecoach stop in 1723, the Hanover Tavern housed and fed many of Patrick Henry's fellow subversives. People like Thomas Jefferson, the Marquis de Lafayette, and George Washington slept here. In fact, Lafayette's recorded journals show that he and Washington slept here at least three times.

But in 1781 British strategists Lord Cornwallis and Colonel Tarleton made the building their headquarters for more than two weeks while preparing for their defeat at Yorktown.

ADDRESS: Route 301, Hanover, Virginia 23069. It's about 13 miles north of Richmond; take the Hanover-Route 54 Exit from I-95

TELEPHONE: 804-798-6547

FACILITIES: Dining and theater; buffet open from 6 to 8 p.m., although it is recommended to arrive by 7:30 p.m.

RESERVATIONS: Required for dining and theater

DRESS: Informal

CREDIT CARDS: None

The tavern was purchased in 1953 by six struggling actors, who had to borrow on the down payment. The tavern became the home of the Barksdale Theater, which still offers the people of the Richmond area a wide array of superbly performed theatrical productions that range from Tennessee Williams' *A Streetcar Named Desire* to the rowdy World War II classic *Mister Roberts*.

Today, the theater is directed, managed, and has much of its settings built by the only remaining member of the original six, David Kilgore, who lives with his family in the old inn.

Performances with dinner are provided year round, Wednesday through Saturday. Although meals are optional, you should take advantage of the bountiful country cooking prior to curtain time. A single entrée and side dishes that change with each meal are offered. A typical meal might go something like this: hot spiced cider, French onion soup, salad, relish tray, rib steak, baked potato, green beans, hot homemade rolls, beverage, and after-dinner mints. Theater tickets range from $3.50 to $5.50, and dinner is an additional $6.

RUTLEDGE INN
AMHERST, VA.

We enjoyed a restful night above the dining room of the Rutledge Inn, in cozy accommodations with part of the inn's high-peaked roof for our ceiling. The room had stained, rough-sawn planks for paneling and beautiful hand-painted Black Forest furniture. The Rutledge Inn, set among a grove of evergreens and hickory trees, is owned by Frank Hodgkins, an American who fell in love with Europe and with a German fraulein, who is now his wife. The European inns he visited inspired him to start this Bavarian-American inn. Although rustic, the accommodations at the Rutledge Inn are probably much more luxurious than its European counterparts—each room has its own private bath, air conditioning, and heating.

The menu, too, includes a number of Bavarian dishes, but there is a preponderance of American dishes. The *schnitzel, braunschweiger,* and other Bavarian entrées are well prepared, as are the vegetables, which include such traditional dishes as red cabbage and potato dumplings. Dinner for two was about $15.

The campuses of Sweetbriar College and Randolph-Macon are nearby. This would be an ideal stopping place for travelers following Route 60 from Lexington to Richmond, Virginia, or an interesting side trip from Char-

ADDRESS: Amherst, Virginia 24521

TELEPHONE: 804-946-7988

FACILITIES: 4 rooms, dining daily. Breakfast from 7:30 to 11 a.m., lunch from 11:30 a.m. to 2 p.m., a vesper teller (cold plate) from 2 to 6 p.m., dinner from 5 to 10 p.m.

RATES: $20 for double room

RESERVATIONS: Required for rooms and evening meals, not necessary for lunch

DRESS: Nice casual to informal

CREDIT CARDS: American Express, BankAmericard

lottesville, some thirty miles north.

SMITHFIELD INN
SMITHFIELD, VA.

After fighting the crowds and the astronomical prices of Williamsburg on the day after Christmas, I found myself driving a car filled with my wife, her parents, her sister and brother-in-law. The six of us watched the tidewater Virginia countryside slip lazily by. We crossed the James River on the Highway 31 ferry and turned left in Surry on Highway 10, heading south past the Surry Nuclear Power Station to Smithfield and the Smithfield Inn. The inn is managed by Smithfield Foods, famous for its Virginia hams.

"If you can find Smithfield, you can find the inn," said James Abbott, innkeeper. And so it was as we turned right at the light at Main Street.

The food in the inn's dining rooms is incredibly good and inexpensive. We were seated in the garden room and served by a gregarious and competent young waitress. We started the meal with appetizers, half of us having the Brunswick stew, the other half marinated pear halves. The stew was spicy and full of vegetables and chicken. It was a welcome contrast to a tasteless watery concoction of the same name that I had been served in Williamsburg for lunch that same day. The pears were enjoyed, as they fizzed "like ginger ale" according to my sister-in-law.

ADDRESS: Main Street, Smithfield, Virginia 23430. Take Jamestown ferry from Williamsburg to Surry; go south on Route 10 about 20 miles

TELEPHONE: 804-357-4358

FACILITIES: Six rooms; lunch Monday through Saturday from 11:30 a.m. to 2 p.m.; dinner Monday through Thursday from 5 to 8:30 p.m., Friday and Saturday until 9 p.m., Sundays noon until 8:30 p.m.

RATES: $22 to $32 for a double room

RESERVATIONS: Required

DRESS: Nice casual during the day, informal in the evening

CREDIT CARDS: American Express, Master Charge

The main dishes were delicious—broiled king crab claws, stuffed crab, sautéed trout, turkey and dressing, and Smithfield ham. The homemade biscuits and griddle cornbread were positively addictive. Peach cobbler and coffee and tea ended the meal. The most incredible aspect of the meal was its cost—six people ate full-course dinners for $50, including a 20 percent tip for the unusually high-quality service.

But there always seems to be a flaw, and at Smithfield it's the rooms. Although the inn was built in 1752, none of the original décor has been retained in the rooms, which are now filled with characterless furniture. The carpet is stained and worn, paint peels from the ceiling, and the wall bulges from inexpertly made plaster repairs thinly veiled by a coat of institutional green paint. Pictures with cracked glass, dirty bathrooms, and inadequate bathroom linens make this a place to avoid as an overnight spot.

However, the lobby of the inn is very nicely furnished with original paintings, antiques, and a most unusual antique doll collection at Christmas time.

The Isle of Wight Courthouse, with its arcaded porch and rounded brick courtroom, is located next door. It dates from 1750. Also nearby are other eighteenth-century buildings—the Gaming House, the Clerk's Office, and the County Jail.

THE TIDES LODGE
IRVINGTON, VA.

Northern Neck is the nether land of Virginia, a fig-shaped bite of land bounded by the Potomac River on the north, the Rappahannock on the south, and the Chesapeake Bay on the east. The highways are uncrowded and unhurried, stretching for miles between small settlements with names like Lively (which isn't) and Irvington.

The Tides Lodge is located just outside the small hamlet of Irvington and just across Carter's Creek from its older sibling, The Tides Inn. But the gulf between the two establishments is much greater than the actual distance across the water. Whereas the Inn is a large, formal resort, the Lodge is a small, less formal, activity-oriented, and above all, friendly little place.

Although the Lodge bills golf as its main attraction, a non-golfer can find plenty to do—tennis, boating, jogging, skeet shooting, swimming, fishing, and more. The golf course was designed by Sir Guy Campbell, the Scotsman from St. Andrews whose course architecture is world renowned. In his honor, the Lodge has taken on a Scottish look, with plaid rugs and waitresses outfitted in the Stewart or Royal Stewart tartan. Even the bellman's necktie is Stewart plaid.

There are a total of forty rooms in the lodge, set in

ADDRESS: Irvington, Virginia 22480. Take Route 3 to Route
646; go west on 646 until just past Christ Church and turn left.
The entrance to the Lodge is well marked
TELEPHONE: 804-438-2233
FACILITIES: 40 rooms and dining available from March
through November. Food served daily from 3 p.m. until 10 p.m.
in The Binnacle; from 8 to 10 a.m. and from noon to 9 p.m.
in main dining room
RATES: Modified American Plan (breakfast and dinner
included with room). Our double room with the **MAP** cost
$70 per day
RESERVATIONS: Recommended
DRESS: Casual during day, informal at night
CREDIT CARDS: None

two rustic buildings. The rough-sawn fir siding of the
buildings blends with the forest of laurel and oak and
pine that surrounds them. Each room has a TV and its
own very private balcony, and nearly every room has a
view of the water through the trees. It's a treat to take
breakfast on the balcony, and its costs only a dollar extra.

The Lodge has two places to dine: the main dining
room and the Binnacle. The main dining room is a more
formal eating area. The Binnacle, in contrast, is a mush-
room-looking, glassed-in gazebo, with an outside wooden
deck set up on stilts to overlook the water and the piers
full of boats. The menu is more limited at the Binnacle
than at the main dining room, but the same high standards of preparation prevail whether you choose sautéed
crabmeat, scallops, or steaks. The hot German potato
salad at the Binnacle is wonderful. Service personnel here
are more informal and friendlier than at the main dining
room.

While you are in the area, be sure to stop at Christ
Church. It is one of the best examples of an eighteenth-
century country church and has been carefully restored
with the help of archeologists. Another significant historic attraction is Stratford Hall, just off Route 3 about
forty miles south of Fredericksburg. This is the Lee
family homestead. Two signers of the Declaration of
Independence were born here, including Richard Henry
Lee, who introduced the motion for independence in the
Continental Congress. "Light Horse" Harry Lee was
the author of George Washington's famous epitaph,
"First in war, first in peace, and first in the hearts of his

countrymen.'' His son, Robert Edward, was General of the Armies of the Confederacy.

The magnificent H-shaped home, with its two clusters of four chimneys, is the most interesting and unique of all the old Virginia homes. An old mill has been restored and grinds corn that is for sale at the small gift shop. Cider and cookies are served in the restored kitchen. All of the outbuildings, or dependencies, have been restored as have the stables. The birthplaces of George Washington and James Monroe are also nearby, although they aren't as elaborate.

SHENANDOAH VIRGINIA

From Winchester to Salem, the Shenandoah section of Virginia is a dramatic mix of valley and mountains. The Skyline Drive and Blue Ridge Parkway mark the eastern edge of this section, the West Virginia border marks the western edge. Running down the center, stringing together the small towns and scenic attractions, is Interstate 81.

But Shenandoah is much more than a place. It is a haunting reminder of things past: tumbling stone fences far from the road, apple trees planted a century ago, plowed fields full of Civil War shrapnel, and arrowheads from long-gone Indian tribes.

The 4,000-foot peaks of the Blue Ridge Mountains and the jagged rock Allegheny Plateau have many hiking trails that are perfect for the short hour-long hike or the week-long wilderness backpack. Antiques, wildlife, and scenic wonders such as the Natural Bridge near Lexington are all part of enjoying the Shenandoah.

In the winter, campers turn into skiers headed for downhill and cross-country areas throughout the mountains. While the hearty head for the slopes, the pampered bask in the luxury of places like the Homestead, built around the warm mineral springs. Craft fairs in Front Royal, pilgrimages to Robert E. Lee's crypt in Lexington, and an old stone and water mill that grinds grain at Mabry's Mill are among the things this unique region offers. The transportation museum in Roanoke has everything from dog sleds to locomotives—a delight for children and adults alike. In May, the Apple Blossom Festival in Winchester is a nationwide event to celebrate the task begun by Johnny Appleseed.

The best way to see the Shenandoah is to take Route 11 rather than Interstate 81. It is more scenic, the traffic is lighter, and you can travel at a more leisurely pace.

ALEXANDER-WITHROW HOUSE
LEXINGTON, VA.

The Alexander-Withrow House is an architectural gem located in the historic town of Lexington, home of Washington and Lee University. The Virginia Military Institute, founded in 1839, and Lee Chapel, in which Light Horse Harry Lee, his son Robert E. Lee, and several other members of the Lee family are buried, are two other historic landmarks. You can get information on these and other attractions at the visitor center, which is located a block and a half from the Alexander-Withrow House. The visitor center will also supply you with a permit to park in any legitimate parking space for as long as you want without getting a ticket.

Built in 1787 by William Alexander, the massive three-story Alexander-Withrow House is unique in the Shenandoah Valley, because it was designed and built with more sophistication than were most structures of that period. The four corner chimneys, the Italianate roof, and the elaborate diamond-shaped patterns in the brickwork are features that distinguish it from other buildings in the valley. The thick brick and masonry walls were probably responsible for the house being one of the few structures to survive a devastating fire that consumed Lexington in 1796.

ADDRESS: 3 Washington Street, Lexington, Virginia 24450
(at the corner of Washington and Main Streets)
TELEPHONE: 703-463-2044 or 463-3268
FACILITIES: 5 suites, lodging only
RATES: $25 for a double room
RESERVATIONS: Required far in advance
DRESS: Casual
CREDIT CARDS: None

The house was the site of Lexington's first school, its first bank, and, since William Alexander was the town's first postmaster, its first post office. The house was a shambles when it was purchased in 1970 by the Historic Lexington Foundation, which restored the exterior and then sold the building to Harriet and Carlson Thomas, who restored the interior. There are now five guest suites, decorated in period style with beautiful antiques and reproductions. Although each suite includes a full-sized living room with a fireplace, a bedroom, a bath, and a kitchenette, the rates are a modest $25 for a double room.

Mrs. Thomas runs an antique shop on the ground floor of the house, and most of the furnishings in the rooms are for sale as well.

No meals are served, but there are a number of good restaurants within two blocks of the house, and there is a small bakery next door that will deliver pastries to your room for breakfast every morning except Sunday. A coffee pot, instant coffee, and tea are provided in the room's kitchenette.

BATTLETOWN INN
BERRYVILLE, VA.

Located on the main street in Berryville, the Battletown Inn is a rambling white frame house surrounded by a monstrous privet hedge. The building itself is somewhat of a town landmark; it was built shortly after the end of the Civil War. It has been operated as an inn, although without lodging, for the past thirty years.

We sat by a window, which looked out on an alley running between the inn and a Georgian brick building. We could see sparrows darting through the wind, and a colorful mountain ash tree (not a true ash) with its berries brilliant orange against its dark green leaves and its boughs moving with the breeze.

The dining rooms of the inn are a series of spaces that ramble along the front and around the side of the building. The décor, though a cut above the typical small town café, is nonetheless undistinguished, with linoleum floors and new colonial-style furnishings. The people, not the furnishings, really make the atmosphere here.

The Battletown Inn serves Southern standards, accompanied by wonderful vegetables; if I were a vegetable, this is where I'd like to be since so much care is given to them. I ordered a vegetable plate that consisted of fried eggplant, baked yellow squash, parslied potatoes, and

ADDRESS: Intersection of Routes 340 and 7, Berryville, Virginia 22611
TELEPHONE: 703-955-1348
FACILITIES: Dining only; Tuesday through Sunday from noon to 8 p.m.
RESERVATIONS: Not required for lunch, but recommended for evening meals
DRESS: Nice casual
CREDIT CARDS: None

candied sweet potatoes. They were delicious by themselves or as an accessory to the smothered chicken, ham, steaks, shad roe, or other house specialties.

The meal started with hot, homemade rum buns and a relish dish of watermelon pickles and apple butter. It ended with light and creamy pecan pie. A dinner for two cost $12.

The apple butter, rum buns, watermelon pickles, pecan pie, salad dressings, and three types of soups are all homemade and are available to take home at very reasonable prices.

BAVARIAN CHEF
MADISON, VA.

O ctober is definitely the best time to visit the Bavarian Chef. Oktoberfest is roughly equivalent to our Fourth of July, Veterans Day, Labor Day, and New Year's Eve all rolled into one. Beer and wurst and schnitzel are the feast of the fest, and since Germany is the beer capital of the world and Bavaria is the beer keg of Germany, what better place to be for Oktoberfest than someplace Bavarian?

From the road, the Bavarian Chef in Madison is not impressive, with pseudo-Bavarian chalet architecture surrounded by a parking lot. But inside this unimposing building is possibly the best German restaurant south of Lüchow's in New York City.

As we walked inside, we went from the rather stark exterior to a rustically paneled entryway and a dining room paneled with rough-sawn lumber. Every window is a different stained-glass window that was specially made for the building. There are two other dining rooms, more formal with wallpapered walls and cuckoo clocks.

Bruni Thalwitz was our hostess. She is co-owner with her husband, Eckhard, who is also the chef. And what a chef! Eckhard was apprenticed as a cook at age thirteen in his native Bavaria in 1950. From there he attended the famous culinary college in Lausanne, Swit-

ADDRESS: Route 29 five miles south of Madison, Virginia 22727. (It is twenty-five miles north of Charlottesville)
TELEPHONE: 703-948-6505
FACILITIES: Dining only; Wednesday through Sunday from 11 a.m. to 11 p.m.
RESERVATIONS: Not necessary for lunch, required for dinner
DRESS: Nice casual to informal
CREDIT CARDS: None, but personal checks are accepted

zerland; practiced his internship in Vevey, Switzerland; and was a chef in Cannes, Casablanca, and Tangier before coming to the United States in 1961.

We started with homemade bread and onion soup that was so thick with cheese and onions that it was almost an onion and cheese stew. It was liberally laced with paprika, which gave it a most unusual and spicy flavor.

We were not really prepared for the Falstaffian quantities of the food we received, but we did our best to finish. I was never sorrier to leave food on my plate than I was that night. Heaping portions of red cabbage and *spatzle* accompanied my plate of *schweineschnitzel,* a dish of fried pork roast slices in a gravy sauce. My wife's plate of *munchener weisswurst* was similarly packed with vegetables. We finished the meal with a Bavarian nut ball (ice cream rolled in nuts and coconut) and *Schwarzwalderkirsche torte* (Black Forest cake), which has alternating layers of chocolate cake soaked in kirsch, cherries, and whipped cream.

Though there are a few American dishes for the unadventurous, the menu offers a wide selection of traditional Bavarian entrées, vegetables, and desserts. We paid $18 for dinner for two.

DANNER HOUSE
MIDDLETOWN, VA.

The floors wave and slant a bit after resting in Middletown for more than 200 years. Three generations of Danners have lived in the house—the first, Jacob Danner, was Middletown's first postmaster (two of his sons became the second and third). Today, the Danner House, with its walls of huge white pine logs and its native limestone fireplaces, is one of the finest restaurants in the Shenandoah Valley.

We were greeted at the door by a woman in colonial costume, who escorted us into a room with a unique double fireplace and seated us at a table in front of the crackling fire. The walls are stripped of their inner coverings to reveal the huge logs with the adz marks still visible, and the wide plank floors are worn.

We ordered broiled trout and veal cordon bleu. Both came well prepared, although the ham in the veal cordon bleu was a bit gristly. The vegetable that accompanied the meal and the tossed salad were routine, but the chicken soup that served as an appetizer was homemade and delicious. The crowning achievement of the meal was diet-shattering pecan pie, hot and baked in the Danner House kitchen. Like the Wayside Inn just down the street, Danner House serves small, hot loaves of bread with the meals. Dinner for two cost $20.

ADDRESS: Route 11 in Middletown, Virginia 22645. Take I-81, Exit 77
TELEPHONE: 703-869-1775
FACILITIES: Dining only, daily from 11:30 a.m. to 9 p.m.
RESERVATIONS: Recommended
DRESS: Informal
CREDIT CARDS: BankAmericard and Master Charge

It is not surprising that some things at the Danner House resemble those at the Wayside Inn, because one of the Danner House owners, Mrs. Carolyn Hammack, was innkeeper at the Wayside Inn for ten years. She oversaw and directed most of the renovation and restoration that upgraded the Wayside Inn after its present owner purchased it. Most of the antiques that sit in its halls and rooms were selected by her.

She left Middletown in 1971 to manage motels and inns in Florida and West Virginia, but returned in 1974. "Well, this is just home to me," she explained. "It's not easy to leave a lifetime, and we found we just didn't feel we belonged anywhere else."

The Danner House has no provisions for overnight lodging, so we reluctantly left its warmth and hospitality and walked back to our room at the Wayside Inn.

GRAVES MOUNTAIN LODGE
SYRIA, VA.

The word bucolic was invented, I'm quite sure, with the sole purpose of describing Graves Mountain Lodge. A visit to the lodge in Syria—with its hearty, farm-cooked meals and beautiful Blue Ridge Mountain scenery—is at least a temporary way of returning to a more relaxing and more basic way of life.

Graves Mountain Lodge was a farm long before it became an inn, and it continues to be an active farm whose fruits provide breakfasts, lunches, and dinners for the lodge guests.

The Graves family settled this pocket of the Blue Ridge back when it was still possible to name a mountain after yourself. Today, inn guests can sit in a rocker on the front porch of the lodge and look across the valley at Graves Mountain. To the east is the apple-sorting shed of the Graves Apple Company, the largest building in the valley. The little fork in the road, suitably decorated with a general store, is the town of Syria, and the trout stream that parallels the road and runs through the front yard of the lodge is the Rose River.

The family started their business in the Depression by taking in boarders. When they needed more space, they acquired several old log cabins built along the Rose River and later built others. Along the way, they constructed

ADDRESS: Route 670 in Syria, Virginia 22743. Take Route 29, then go west on Route 231 to Madison. Take 231 five miles to Route 670, turn left and go four miles to the lodge
TELEPHONE: 703-923-4231
FACILITIES: 21 rooms, 11 cabins; dining room open daily for breakfast from 8:30 to 9:30 a.m., lunch from 12:30 to 1:30 p.m. except Sunday when it is served from 1 to 2:30 p.m., and dinner from 6:30 to 7:30 p.m. Closed November to April
RATES: Around $25 per day for meals and lodgings
RESERVATIONS: Required far in advance
DRESS: Casual
CREDIT CARDS: BankAmericard

the mess hall that feeds guests family style at dozens of long tables, and a lodge unit up the hill in the peach orchard.

After a day of playing tennis, hiking in nearby Shenandoah National Park, horseback riding, swimming, fishing, or engaging in the lodge's premier activity—being lazy—the home-cooked meals are a delight. Nothing fancy, mind you. Apples when they are in season, corn when it's ready, vegetables as they reach their prime, and as much other home-grown food as the huge farm will produce. This is not the place for people who want to be alone. Seating is eight to each rectangular pine table. Second and third helpings are encouraged and frequently taken. The only house rule is not to take more than you can eat. Fried chicken, scalloped potatoes, steak, summer squash, peach cobbler, apple dumplings, beans, homemade bread—the list is as endless as the amount of weight you can gain.

The recreation room has games and the only television in the lodge. For large groups, the cabins are the most suitable; for couples, either the lodge or the farmhouse is best. The cost includes meals and rarely runs more than $25 per day per person.

GRISTMILL SQUARE
WARM SPRINGS, VA.

It's hard to know exactly what to call Gristmill Square in Warm Springs. It's a restaurant with two sumptuous suites for rent, a pottery shop, an antique shop, an art gallery, and a wide range of other shops including a women's clothing store and a country store. It is a combination of Williamsburg restoration, Disneyland whimsy, and Georgetown shopping.

Gristmill Square's creator and owner is Philip Hirsh. After retiring from a distinguished career as a corporation president, Hirsh lived on his sailboat for three years with his wife, Catherine, and then returned to his 2,000-acre farm just outside Warm Springs to "decide what to do with the rest of our lives."

It was then that he noticed the old gristmill, circa 1771, that was still grinding away. He bought the mill, all the outbuildings surrounding it, a house across the street and one next door. Soon, with the addition of two two-bedroom suites, the Water Wheel Restaurant turned into an inn offering overnight lodgings. Philip and Catherine Hirsh still plan to add twelve more lodging rooms, a tennis court, a swimming pool, and other amenities that will make this a miniature resort.

The Water Wheel Restaurant is Philip's favorite part of the development; he can often be found in the

ADDRESS: Just off Route 220 in Warm Springs, Virginia
24484
TELEPHONE: 703-839-2231
FACILITIES: Two suites; dining in the Water Wheel
Restaurant Tuesday through Sunday from noon to 2:30 p.m.,
and from 6 to 9 p.m. Shops open weekdays from 10 a.m. to
5 p.m.
RATES: Single daily rate for the tower suite is $32.50, for the
Main Street suite, $27.50. Each additional person is $6 more
RESERVATIONS: Required way in advance for lodgings;
appreciated but not usually necessary for dinner
DRESS: Nice casual to informal for dinner, casual for lunch
CREDIT CARDS: American Express, BankAmericard, Carte
Blanche, Diner's Club, and Master Charge

kitchen showing his chef how to cook. And he's done an
excellent job of teaching, as the food reflects. Our dinner
started with *vichyssoise* and salad, followed by filet
mignon with wine sauce, fresh corn on the cob, and homemade bread. It ended with a *flan* (caramel custard).
Everything was perfect: the *vichyssoise* was creamy and
smooth, with a sprinkling of chives on the top; the salad
was imaginative, with carrots, beets, and other vegetables
spicing up the routine lettuce and tomato; the filet was
cooked to perfection, and the light wine sauce enhanced
but did not overpower the taste of the meat. Dinner for
two cost $38.

Philip Hirsh gave away most of the machinery that
was in the mill: the Smithsonian Institution in Washington, and the Hegley Museum of Power in Wilmington,
Delaware, both acquired pieces. With most of the work-
ings gone, the cozy nooks, the huge exposed timbers, and
the many dining levels give a sense of privacy and intimacy in which to enjoy the meal. Although the unusual
overshot wheel still turns, it no longer provides power for
the day-to-day work of grinding grain.

There is an amply stocked wine cellar with primarily
American labels in the basement of the Water Wheel.
Even if you are not a wine lover, you'll want to walk
down after your meal to examine some of the machinery
that is left and admire the design of the room, on which
the Hirshes have lavished more care than many restaura-
teurs do on their dining rooms.

Reservations for lodgings must be made far in advance since there are only two suites. The tower apartment—which has a turreted, circular living room with tiles laid in a spiral starting from the center—is a masterpiece. Since both suites have two bedrooms, it is an ideal place to come with friends. Both suites also have fireplaces, completely equipped kitchens, a washer and dryer, and daily maid service, as well as a balcony or outside deck. Available nearby are golf, tennis, horseback riding, fishing, hiking, skiing, and much more.

The great overshot wheel is powered by warm water that flows from the warm springs just up the hill, and if you want to sample the therapeutic pools, the Hirshes can make arrangements.

HOLLYMEAD INN
CHARLOTTESVILLE, VA.

The Hollymead Inn is a country - cozy colonial inn with food that is as rich as its history. The first part of the Hollymead Inn in Charlottesville was built about 1780 by Hessian soldiers taken prisoner of war in Saratoga, New York, and brought to Charlottesville for safe keeping. When their quarters became overcrowded, they were ordered to build what is now the Hessian room of the Hollymead. A second portion of the inn was built when the building was used as a boy's school after the turn of the nineteenth century, and the final portion was added in 1937 when the entire inn was renovated and restored.

We started our meal with peanut soup, which was light and—with chunks of carrots and green beans—more like a vegetable chowder, with a taste that resembled boiled peanuts. If you go here, somebody in your party should order it even if the idea of peanut soup doesn't appeal to you. It will after you taste it.

Our tiny table for two was by the fireplace in the Hessian Room, although there was no fire that night. We sampled the relish dish and the variety of hot muffins as we watched groups of people arrive and depart. Most looked to us to be either professorial types or families visiting their children at the nearby University of Vir-

ADDRESS: The east side of Route 29, about six miles from Charlottesville, Virginia 22901. The entrance is not well marked and you may miss it if traveling south on 29. If you cross the Rivanna River traveling south, you've gone too far

TELEPHONE: 804-973-8488

FACILITIES: Dining only; Tuesday through Sunday starting at 5 p.m. Closed Mondays, Christmas Eve, Christmas Day, and New Year's Day

RESERVATIONS: Required

DRESS: Nice casual to informal

CREDIT CARDS: BankAmericard and Master Charge

ginia.

Beef seemed to be the Hollymead Inn's forte, so I ordered the specialty of the evening—beef Wellington—and Shan ordered a ribeye steak.

The beef Wellington was tender and well seasoned, and the meat was choice. The pâté was very mild and sweet. Shan's steak, which came tender and done to her instructions, went well with the delicious batter-fried mushrooms she ordered.

Dessert is always my favorite course, and it is a pleasure to find someone who does it well. I had Irish coffee pie, which could make a leprechaun out of a Welshman. Shan had strawberry pie with fresh strawberries. There is a large variety of homemade desserts to choose from, and it seems unlikely that you could make a bad choice.

The service was prompt, friendly, and attentive, and we were not rushed through any of the courses. Our dinner for two cost $28.

MICHIE TAVERN
CHARLOTTESVILLE, VA.

Located just a few hundred yards from Monticello, on land sold to John Michie by Major John Henry (Patrick Henry's father), Michie Tavern is 230 years of history and a great place to eat lunch.

After the land for the tavern was transferred to Michie in 1746, he established an ordinary that fed and bedded some of the most famous of our founding fathers: President James Monroe entertained General Lafayette there; General Andrew Jackson (later to be President) stopped there on his way to Washington flush with victory after the battle of New Orleans; and Thomas Jefferson also entertained there on occasion.

Today, the inn is both a museum and a restaurant, and is a "must" stop for the visitor to Monticello.

From the outside, the tavern is an imposing structure that has been added to several times. The main part, with its side chimney and covered two-story front porch, is a classic rendition of the southern ordinary architecture that one sees more frequently the further south one travels.

Michie Tavern has an eclectic collection of revolutionary items, including Mr. Michie's personal flintlock rifle (with which he presumably kept order on Friday nights), colonial gadgets of all sorts, and some rare co-

ADDRESS: Charlottesville, Virginia 22901, about a quarter of a mile downhill from the entrance to Monticello
TELEPHONE: 804-977-1234
FACILITIES: Dining only; daily from 11:30 a.m. to 3 p.m.
RESERVATIONS: Not accepted, but crowds here are caused by the number of visitors and bus tours that visit Monticello, especially in the summertime. If you expect to eat without waiting an inordinate amount of time, arrive about 11 a.m. and stand by the door
DRESS: Casual
CREDIT CARDS: None

lonial furnishing including much of the tavern's original furniture.

The tavern serves surprisingly good food for a place that caters primarily to the non-returning tourist trade. Meals are served in a converted log slave house that is nearly as old as the tavern. The menu is strictly southern country fare and does not vary: blackeyed peas, stewed tomatoes, cole slaw, green bean salad, homemade cornbread and biscuits, curd cheese, potato salad, and fried chicken. Lunch for two was $9.

Hopefully, lunch at Michie Tavern will put those who've just come from visiting Monticello back in a good mood. The people at Monticello manage to turn a tour of an architectural gem into an impersonal cattle train operation. A family in front of us waiting in line together for the house tour was separated into two groups rather abruptly when the officious person at the front door slammed the door in the face of the grandmother of the group. She was prevented from entering, and the rest of her family were prevented from getting back out. Jefferson would not have tolerated such rudeness in his home.

NARROW PASSAGE INN
WOODSTOCK, VA.

It looks like what 10,000 roadside diners in America try to imitate and fail. There's no good way to imitate with concrete and plastic the look and feel of irregular fieldstones gathered from open pastures and meadows, and pieced together like a jigsaw puzzle into a wall.

The fieldstone walls are what distinguishes the outside of the Narrow Passage Inn in Woodstock from that of the usual roadside diner. The inn, which was built in 1927, is also set apart by its deserved reputation for serving the best seafood in western Virginia.

We passed through the small entry alcove and walked alongside the skiff that dominates the center of the main dining room and is used as a salad bar. We were seated at the rear of the dining room by windows with a beautiful view of the Shenandoah River and of Massanutten Mountain. Because the weather was warm and sunny, the stone fireplace lay idle. But on a gray wintry day, this would be a perfect place to warm by the fire.

We started the meal with hot rum buns, freshly baked and dripping with delicious rum frosting. After salad, we enjoyed our entrées—broiled filet of sole and crab imperial. It is difficult to find fish that is as fresh and as well prepared. We finished our meal with the cob-

ADDRESS: Route 11 just outside of Woodstock, Virginia 22664
TELEPHONE: 703-459-4770 .
FACILITIES: Dining only; Tuesday through Friday from 11:30 a.m. to 8:30 p.m., Saturdays noon to 9 p.m. Closed in winter
RESERVATIONS: Not required
DRESS: Nice casual
CREDIT CARDS: American Express and Master Charge

bler of the day—apple. Salad, rum buns, dessert, and beverage are all included in the fixed price meals, which range from $3.50 to $9.25.

THE OLD MILL
STRASBURG, VA.

Running an inn is an act of love. George Pappas knows that—he labored at his love, The Old Mill Inn in Strasburg, for thirty-eight years. Pappas wanted to be sure his inn was in good hands before he retired to Florida.

He found the right hands: Joe and Elizabeth Fisher. The young couple are lifelong residents of the Strasburg area and had always admired The Old Mill. It was a dream come true when they finally bought it in September 1976.

"Well, Mr. Pappas really didn't want to sell it . . . and he wasn't just going to sell it to anyone," Mrs. Fisher told me as we walked through the lower level of the mill to inspect the great gears and machinery that once ground grain. "In fact, after we'd bought it, we got calls every now and then from him saying 'If you've changed your mind, I've still got the money in my pocket.' But of course we'd have been crazy to change our mind."

As I walked in—the first time since it had reopened under its new management—I noticed some subtle differences. Nothing that tinkered with the charm and character I'd fallen in love with a year before, but some little touches. Red and white checked linen tablecloths and curtains that splash a bit of light into the huge, dark

ADDRESS: Route 11, Strasburg, Virginia 22657
TELEPHONE: 703-465-5980
FACILITIES: Dining only; Monday, Wednesday, and Thursday from noon to 8 p.m.; Friday, Saturday, and Sunday until 10 p.m. Closed Tuesdays
RESERVATIONS: Not necessary, except for Friday and Saturday nights
DRESS: Nice casual
CREDIT CARDS: None

stone and wood dining hall, kerosene lanterns on each table—not the electrified kind, but the real thing—and some minor rearrangement of furniture and tidying up of walls and shelves. The changes are just the sort of thing that George Pappas would have done in his more energetic days.

But some things have remained the same. The rough-stone corner fireplace and the two-foot thick stone walls and hand-hewn beams are still the same, and the same chef—the only one the inn has ever had since it opened in 1938—is there preparing the same delicious food. The warmth and friendliness are also still there. Even the stories that George Pappas told the townspeople about the inn are now told by patrons and friends. Like the story about how the inn was saved from being burned during Sheridan's march through the Shenandoah Valley. A main strategy of the Union forces was to starve out the rebels; therefore, mills were prime targets. But The Old Mill—built about 1755—was saved from the torch by the amorous exploits of the miller's daughters with General Sheridan and his officers.

The Old Mill serves standard country fare, such as ham, fried chicken, and steaks. I talked with a couple of patrons while I was there and they said that the steaks were "out of this world." I stopped by for lunch on a bright blue but frigid January day, and as I looked over the menu I spotted barbecue.

"Tell me about the barbecue," I asked the waitress. "Well . . ." she thought a moment and then, realizing that I was from out of town and couldn't have heard about it word of mouth, said, "About all I can say is that it's homemade and full of chunks and delicious." She was right. It was huge, on a mammoth bun that must have been baked by a bionic *boulanger*.

The French fries that came with it harkened back to the days of yore when knights were knights and potatoes were potatoes. They are made from fresh potatoes that are cut fresh with each order. I got an entire potato.

The only thing better than the food here is the price. My huge BBQ, fries, beverage, and dessert cost an outrageous $2.35.

SKY CHALET
MT. JACKSON, VA.

The Sky Chalet in the Blue Ridge Mountains near Mount Jackson is the kind of place that brings back memories of visiting your grandmother living in the country. As I rocked in my chair on the porch, listening to the strains from the piano as another guest played, the mountain breezes gently wafted through the maples. Somewhere in the valley a pair of headlights snaked its way along a dirt road. The piano stopped and was replaced with the litany of night creatures, hooting and swishing their nocturnal lines.

The Sky Chalet is just that—a chalet. The rustic interior has natural varnished wood tones and massive structural beams that frame the stone fireplace in the dining room. The huge living room is filled with comfortable overstuffed chairs, two sofas, and an upright piano. Each evening, Mrs. Joseph Wright, who has run the Sky Chalet for nearly thirty years, holds court in the dining room and chats with her guests as she plays solitaire.

The Sky Chalet has six rooms and three cottages. If you're not an inn guest you still may eat here, but you should make reservations the day before. Meals are served family style. Mrs. Wright is always proud to announce that she has never served a slice of store-bought bread to her guests. The cooking is home style—

ADDRESS: Route 263 about 10 miles west of Mt. Jackson, Virginia 22842. Take Exit 68 off of I-81 and go north on Route 11 to its intersection with Route 263 in Mt. Jackson; or take Exit 69 and travel south on Route 11 to the intersection
TELEPHONE: 703-856-2147
FACILITIES: Six rooms and three cottages; dining every day, breakfast from 8:30 to 9 a.m., lunch at 1 p.m., and dinner at 6 p.m.
RATES: Overnight stay with dinner and breakfast cost $35 for two
RESERVATIONS: Recommended for lodgings; required for diners who are not guests
DRESS: Casual to blue jeans
CREDIT CARDS: None

ham and chicken, steaks, plenty of fresh vegetables, and homemade desserts. Our overnight stay with dinner and breakfast cost $35.

The Sky Chalet has a swimming pool for the energetic, hiking trails for the ambitious, and hammocks strung between shady maple trees for the lazy. The recreation room has Ping Pong and a pool table, and the Bryce ski slopes are only a ten-minute drive away.

THE WAYSIDE INN
MIDDLETOWN, VA.

The sun was chasing away the remains of the New Year's Eve snow that had lightly dusted the Blue Ridge Mountains. The warmth that greeted us in the main entrance of the Wayside Inn in Middletown was a welcome respite from that January 1 cold, which tightened coat collars and delighted skiers. We noticed several cars with skis racked on top, ready for the slopes nearby.

The inn was built in 1797 and served as a stagecoach stop on the Shenandoah Valley Turnpike. Its main drawing card now is its furnishings—unusual antiques and collectibles. The French gentleman's washstand in the living room is a most unusual piece, with a blue glazed porcelain basin, brass fixtures, mahogany case, and an ingenious system for creating running water. Also interesting is a weathered chunk of wood that has a notarized certificate attached to its case attesting that it is a piece of the cherry tree that young George Washington is said to have chopped down. Other memorabilia include a telegram from John D. Rockefeller, Jr., reserving a room for him in 1922.

The rooms are undoubtedly more comfortable and better furnished now than they were when the tycoon stayed here, due to the efforts of Washington, D.C., attor-

ADDRESS: Route 11 in Middletown, Virginia 22645, 15 miles south of Winchester. Take I-81, Exit 77
TELEPHONE: 703-869-1797
FACILITIES: 21 rooms; dining Monday through Saturday from 7 a.m. to 9 p.m., Sundays noon to 9 p.m.
RATES: $16 to $25
RESERVATIONS: Recommended, especially for Saturday nights
DRESS: Nice casual in the day, informal at dinner
CREDIT CARDS: American Express, BankAmericard, and Master Charge

ney Leo Bernstein, who purchased the inn in 1960 and added such modern conveniences as private baths and air conditioning and furnished the rooms with antiques or reproductions. Try to avoid rooms number five and six; they are located over a noisy dishwasher.

Meals are served in a wide variety of small, cozy dining rooms by waitresses in colonial costume. However, the food is undistinguished. A small loaf of fresh bread baked on the premises was the high point of our meal. We also enjoyed the peanut soup and the vegetables —black-eyed peas and turnip greens. A typical dinner for two with coffee costs $15, not including the tip.

In general, the personnel are indifferent to their guests' well being. The friendliness experienced in other country inns is missing here. However, it's still worth spending a night to look at the antiques.

NORTHERN VIRGINIA

Northern Virginia is probably best known for being a bedroom community of Washington, D.C., and the home of the CIA, the Pentagon, and huge shopping malls. But there are some green sanctuaries within the suburban sprawl and lovely green countryside as you get further away from Washington.

The Middleburg-Leesburg area is good for spending Saturday and Sunday afternoons driving around and looking at the horses and at the plantations once occupied by the landed Virginia gentry and now more likely to be owned by rich diplomats,

celebrities, and those who want people to think of them as such. Middleburg seems to have more Mercedes, Citroens, and various expensive Italian-made cars per capita than any other town in the United States.

There are reminders of a harsher kind of life—the Civil War battlefields, like the one at Manassas (remember the Battles of Bull Run?) and the historical markers describing the exploits of the Confederate guerrilla fighter Colonel John Mosby, the "Grey Ghost."

Each year, the restored village of Waterford opens its doors to visitors who come to marvel at its quaintness and its beautifully restored buildings, and to participate in its annual craft and folk crafts fair.

Northern Virginia is also the home of Mount Vernon; Old Town Alexandria, which displays its Scottish heritage in its annual Christmas walk in December; a distillery making Lord Fairfax bourbon; a host of restored old mills; the Wolf Trap National Park for the Performing Arts; and Arlington National Cemetery.

J. Wayne Higgs

BLACKBEARD'S INN
OCCOQUAN, VA.

"Occoquan," says Nan Mabry, co-owner of the Cinnamon Cellar handicrafts shop, "is a nifty little town." She's right.

Crammed into a niche on the banks of the Occoquan River, in fact almost directly beneath the bridge that crosses the river, the little town with its old buildings, unique shops, and warm brand of welcome was one of the luckiest discoveries I have ever made.

In stark contrast to commercialized shopping centers, many of the shops in the town are in homes and in former homes, with handmade wares and antiques hanging from the ceiling, stacked in corners, decked out on a board across the bathtub, and stacked on the kitchen drainboard. In this little town that's so small that it almost got left out of the Civil War (history says that a Union gunboat steamed up the Occoquan, fired one shot into the village, and then steamed away when nobody responded), there are no fewer than thirty stores, which sell handmade canvas goods, pastries, plants, carpentered goods, crafts, and antiques. And food.

Blackbeard's Inn occupies the corner of Mill and Union streets just a block from the river and, as is fitting, has a nautical décor. The inn is rather a hobby with its owner, Don Sonner, whose main enterprise is selling

ADDRESS: Union Street, Occoquan, Virginia 22125. Take the Route 123 Occoquan Exit from I-95 to the Occoquan turnoff, which is just east of the river bridge. Follow this to Union Street and turn right; Blackbeard's will be on your right in two blocks
TELEPHONE: 703-550-9218
FACILITIES: Dining only; Monday through Saturday from 4 to 10 p.m., Sundays 1 to 9 p.m.
RESERVATIONS: Not required in the day, recommended evenings and Sunday dinners
DRESS: Nice casual in the day, nice casual to informal at night
CREDIT CARDS: BankAmericard and Master Charge

fresh seafood. It's no surprise, then, that the specialties of the house at Blackbeard's are centered around those dishes that once swam rather than those that walked or flew.

The nautical trappings—nets, weathered wood paneling, pulleys, and other accessories—go well in the 100-year-old building, and the meals are served on tables of huge thick slabs of varnished wood. But unlike the wood, the food is plain, unvarnished goodness.

We started with crab soup that was thick with huge pieces of sweet backfin meat. It was topped with whipped cream, which unfortunately was out of a can and too sweet. Discard it before you start.

The seafood platter was delicious—shrimp, oysters, clams, scallops, a crab cake, fried fish, and hush puppies. It was tender, fresh, and cooked to perfection. Dinner for two came to about $16.

Blackbeard's owner, incidentally, lives in the magnificent stone mansion, Rockledge, that can be seen from the main street at the end of the town. It was designed by the same architect as Gunston Hall and was built in 1758 by the owner of the mill, which was the center of industry in Occoquan in those days. The old mill house is located across the road and is now a museum and information center.

CEDAR KNOLL INN
MOUNT VERNON, VA.

Don't dine late at the Cedar Knoll Inn in Mount Vernon or you'll miss one of the most beautiful views available to Washington area diners. If you get there for lunch or for an early dinner, you can enjoy the magnificent sight of the Potomac and of trees and hills that makes you question whether or not you are really *that* close to Washington, D.C.

The main building in the inn was built in 1854 on land that was part of the original farm owned by the Washington family, whose own Mount Vernon home is just another five minutes or so away from the Cedar Knoll Inn.

It's hard to imagine a better place for summertime lunches than the front terrace, which has outdoor dining when the weather permits.

But whether outdoor or in, the dining is perfect anytime. The menu is rather limited, but the preparation of any dish on the menu—from seafood to *wiener schnitzel* to ham and chicken—is excellent. I am a seafood platter freak and theirs was one of the best I've had. Shrimp, bits of sweet backfin crabmeat, scallops, a lobster tail, and clams were all sautéed in butter and served still sizzling. For dessert, you have to order the German buttercream cake with almonds, but have your waitress

ADDRESS: Mount Vernon, Virginia 22121, about six miles south of Alexandria on the Mt. Vernon Parkway
TELEPHONE: 703-360-7880
FACILITIES: Dining only; daily from 11:30 a.m. to 9 p.m.
RESERVATIONS: Required
DRESS: Nice casual for lunch, informal in the evening
CREDIT CARDS: American Express, BankAmericard, Carte Blanche, Diner's Club, and Master Charge

reserve a slice before you get your entrée since it is so popular that there may be none left by the time you finish. Our dinner for two cost $25, including cocktails and dessert.

If you arrive on a sunny summer Saturday or Sunday you're liable to see a wedding, since this picturesque setting is a popular one.

COUNTRY SQUIRE
SEVEN CORNERS, VA.

Imagine how astonished the original owner of the Country Squire in Seven Corners, Virginia, would feel if, after 100 years, he returned to the secluded stone and timber mountain retreat he had built to find it surrounded by six-lane roads, shopping centers, and a maze of highways and roads. The city is definitely catching up to the Country Squire, although the huge spreading elms and the two acres of plants, trees, and shrubs serve as a green barrier to block out the urban world.

When we arrived a cheery fire was burning in the fireplace. The stone chimney dominates the exterior of the inn and the hearth dominates the interior of a small dining room with a high-pitched, open-raftered ceiling and walls covered with so many collectibles that we could hardly tell what kind of walls they were.

We were seated in what used to be a huge screened-in porch and is now the main dining room, some 25-by-50 feet large. The original board and batten exterior walls are painted and decorated with carved wooden animals and original art. Many of the wall decorations we saw were for sale and were supplied by the Velvet Rooster Gift shop in the same building, which carries a wide range of antiques, gifts and whimsies.

Although the main dining room is large, the low

ADDRESS: Patrick Henry Drive, about 150 yards west of Route 7 (Leesburg Pike), Seven Corners, Virginia 22044
TELEPHONE: 703-534-4200
FACILITIES: Dining only; Monday through Saturday from 11:30 a.m. to 2:30 p.m. and from 5:30 to 10 p.m. A champagne brunch is served Saturday and Sunday from 11:30 a.m. to 8:30 p.m.
RESERVATIONS: Recommended
DRESS: Informal
CREDIT CARDS: American Express and Diner's Club

ceiling with exposed beams and occasional supporting posts break up the large space. This, combined with the subdued lighting from a variety of Tiffany-style and country lantern lamps, gives you the feeling of eating on the porch of a wealthy friend's country house.

I started my meal with an onion soup that was homemade but very bland. Shan ordered crab soup, which was seasoned with a gumbo filé that was very tasty. I'd recommend the crab soup, though it was a bit short of crabmeat. The salad was as a salad should be: lettuce, red cabbage, and carrots—well chilled, super crisp, and delightfully shredded (a welcome change from the give-them - huge - chunks - of - lettuce - and - sit - back - and - watch - them - wrestle - with - it school of salad making).

The salad was followed by a delicious steak. Shan's lamb chops were also outstanding. Both the lamb and the filet mignon were prepared in the same manner; grilled over lump charcoal, not briquettes, and seasoned with huge chunks of freshly crushed black pepper; they were tender, tasty, done to perfection, with no excess fat.

Baked potatoes come with the meal, but vegetables are à la carte, and I recommend you order at least one. I ordered broccoli Hollandaise, Shan ordered the sautéed mushrooms; both were well worth the extra cost.

We had to skip dessert for time's sake since service had been extremely slow and very poor. Mrs. Doris Johnson, who is a co-owner with her husband, Leonard, explained after the meal that some of her service personnel had not shown up for work that evening.

A meal for two, including drinks but not including coffee or dessert, cost $27.

EVANS FARM INN
MCLEAN, VA.

The Evans Farm Inn, a reconstruction of an eighteenth-century Virginia plantation, is built of pieces from various farms, mills, and houses that have been torn down to make way for new roads, parking lots, and buildings. Located on forty bucolic acres two miles east of the suburban madness of Tyson's Corners, the inn comes closer to my concept of how The Ideal Country Inn looks than any other one we visited. And though the food is good, it simply doesn't compare to the wonderful architecture and setting.

The antiques and reproductions that furnish the main dining room fit perfectly with the huge hand-hewn beams taken from an old farm, the wide-planked wooden floors, and the waiters and table service personnel, all of whom wear period costumes.

In addition to the main dining room, there's the Evans Mill, made of old timbers from Swink's Mill and Magarity Barn and of foundation stones from the Ravensworth plantation. It also has a Dutch door from Wakefield, the birthplace of George Washington; grindstones from Arlington, Virginia, and from New Market, Maryland; gears and wheels from Haymarket, Virginia; water wheels from Philadelphia; and timbers from Fredericksburg. It is truly a rest home for the remains of old mills.

ADDRESS: 1696 Chain Bridge Road, McLean, Virginia 22101. Take the Route 123 Exit from the George Washington Parkway; or take Exit 11 of I-495 (the Beltway) if you are driving north, Exit 12E if you are traveling south
TELEPHONE: 703-356-8000
FACILITIES: Dining only; Monday through Thursday from noon to 2:30 p.m. and from 5 to 9 p.m., Friday and Saturday until 10 p.m., Sunday dinner served from noon until 9 p.m. Informal meals served in the Sitting Duck Pub, Monday through Friday from 11:30 a.m. to 2 p.m. and from 5 to 11 p.m., Saturday from 5 to 11 p.m.
RESERVATIONS: Not accepted
DRESS: Informal
CREDIT CARDS: American Express and BankAmericard

The stable houses a gift and antiques shop and the cookhouse, behind the main dining room, is available for private parties and functions. The garden, across the road in front of the main building, provides the fresh flowers for table settings and some of the salad greens and vegetables served. The Log Smoke House, used for curing pork, was originally part of the Magarity Farm in McLean.

Horses, goats, and other livestock roam the farm. To see them and the reconstructed mill and buildings, you should arrive in the daylight, either for lunch or for an early dinner.

We started dinner with some of the many relishes available at the salad bar: cranberry-orange sauce, watermelon pickles, apple butter, marinated kidney beans, cottage cheese, and more. We passed up the lettuce salad, which looked a bit tired, but not the fresh baked rye bread, which was still hot from the oven.

The meal itself was a good one. The scallops were sweet and tasty and, though they had been prepared with a standard breading, were not greasy. The roast duck was covered with a bland sauce that didn't do justice to the duck. Tasty spoonbread—an old southern cornmeal dish—was served along with two vegetables.

The desserts—Huguenot cake and apple dumplings—were the best prepared parts of the meal. The dumpling had an entire apple inside the browned pastry and was delicious. The Huguenot cake was filled with pieces of apple and nuts and topped with ice cream. A meal for two, including cocktails and dessert, cost about $20.

GADSBY'S TAVERN
ALEXANDRIA, VA.

Gadsby's Tavern in Old Town Alexandria is a restored historic structure, said to have been the dining place of George Washington and other revolutionary luminaries. It is truly a Bicentennial restaurant —mainly because it takes 200 years to be served. However, it is worth the wait, both for the food and to take in the details of the exquisitely restored interior.

The primary reason for the long waiting time—our party of four had a 9:30 reservation and were seated at 10:20—is the restaurant's practice of scheduling "sittings" instead of reservations. In theory, patrons are supposed to arrive at roughly the same time and depart by a certain hour. This doesn't take into account people who like to linger over dessert or a third cup of coffee.

The Georgian architecture of the building has been faithfully restored to its original elegance. Actually, the tavern is located in two buildings: the Coffee House, which dates from before the Revolution, and the old City Hotel, which was built in 1792. It was threatened with demolition in 1928, but was saved after the Alexandria American Legion bought it for their club. They sold it to the City of Alexandria in 1972. After three years of work, it was once again opened to the imbibing and eating public on George Washington's birthday in 1976.

ADDRESS: 130 North Royal Street, Alexandria, Virginia 22314
TELEPHONE: 703-548-1288
FACILITIES: Dining only; Monday through Saturday from 11:30 a.m. to 2:30 p.m. and 5:30 to 9:30 p.m., Sundays 3 to 9:30 p.m.
RESERVATIONS: Required for sittings
DRESS: Informal
CREDIT CARDS: American Express and BankAmericard

The restorers seem to have captured the richness of the interior décor. They even reproduced the City Hotel's ballroom woodwork, which was scavenged for the American Wing of the Metropolitan Museum of Art in New York when the hotel was threatened with demolition.

According to the restaurant's menu, the tavern was "the setting of brilliant balls for society in the 1700's, meetings of patriots and receptions for at least six Presidents of the United States." Among those who enjoyed the hostelry were the Marquis de Lafayette, John Paul Jones, Baron de Kalb, Aaron Burr, George Mason, Francis Scott Key, and Henry Clay.

Dining in the style of our founding fathers can be a psychological trip for history buffs, and at Gadsby's it's also a culinary delight and surprisingly reasonable considering the price of Washington restaurants. Our party of four ate for about $50 including tip, wine, and dessert, but not including drinks.

The baked fish du jour stuffed with shrimp and crabmeat was prepared to perfection. The roasted duck in Madeira sauce also was well-prepared, moist but not excessively fatty. The menu calls it "General Washington's Favorite Duck," but I doubt if it has really lived to be 200 years old. A rare slab of the roast rib of beef was still available even at the last sitting and was served with Yorkshire pudding and fresh, nose-wrenching horseradish. The veal was sweet and fresh and was complemented by a stuffing lightly seasoned with sage.

The tossed salad and vegetables were unexciting, but the warm, slightly sweet "Sally Lunn" bread was a delight. A perfect accompaniment to the fresh-baked bread is their homemade soup.

The coffee is also excellent, though a bit dear at 50¢ per cup. The menu offers "English Tea Service" for 75¢, but all the diner gets is a pewter-like pot of hot water and a tea bag.

THE GREEN TREE
LEESBURG, VA.

Most everyone knows of Thomas Jefferson as a jack of all cultures— an American DaVinci —but few are aware of his culinary skills. Few, that is, outside of the Green Tree Restaurant in Leesburg, Virginia, where he is the inspirer of the authentic eighteenth-century dishes that are served here. Mrs. Jan Dickson McVay, proprietress of the colonial eating spot just off the square in this restored hamlet, told us that after five years as envoy to Paris, Jefferson returned to the United States with an appreciation of Continental food preparation. This interest, combined with his enjoyment of American food, led to the mixture of European and American cuisine that marks the fare at the Green Tree.

"Mr. Jefferson's kitchen staff was encouraged to use sauces, wines, and herbs in the preparation of foods indigenous to Virginia," Mrs. McVay told us over a cup of coffee one Sunday morning after we had just finished a most unusual eighteenth-century brunch.

"The bill of fare," she continued, "represents both in body and spirit this approach to dining."

More importantly, all of the recipes that are used were carefully researched with the help of historians and records in the National Archives and the Library of

ADDRESS: 15 South King Street, Leesburg, Virginia 22075
TELEPHONE: 703-777-7246
FACILITIES: Dining only; Tuesday through Saturday from 11:30 a.m. to 2:30 p.m. and from 6 to 10 p.m., Mondays 11:30 a.m. to 2:30 p.m. only, Sundays brunch from noon to 4 p.m. and dinner from 6 to 9 p.m.
RESERVATIONS: Recommended
DRESS: Nice casual to informal
CREDIT CARDS: None

Congress. Chef Michael Bose allows no deviations from the recipes, insuring that the dishes taste, feel, and look as close to their historical antecedents as possible.

In a world filled with microwave ovens and electronic gewgaws, where some of Washington's most expensive restaurants turn out dishes tasting like Stouffer's frozen entrées, the Green Tree is a welcome respite.

"If it (the recipe) says to make almond paste by crushing them with a mortar and pestle, then we do it that way," Bose said. "This gives a paste whose texture is filled with odd-sized pieces of nutmeats unobtainable with machines."

This is the only inn in the three-state area covered by this book that offers historically accurate eighteenth-century dining properly prepared. (The inns in Williamsburg make an attempt, but in nearly every case, deviate significantly from the original recipes. In addition, the quality of their food does not compare to that of the Green Tree.)

The Green Tree's menu changes as the seasons change. "We do not choose canned or frozen foods," Mrs. McVay explained. "This means that when the season for oysters ends, so do our oyster pastries. The mint ice cream that we make ourselves has to be replaced with rum and black walnut ice cream when the last of the fresh mint has been picked."

But does this constant seasonal change make things difficult?

"Not at all," she countered. "Something delicious is always coming into season."

While in many historic inns and taverns, the diner sometimes has to overlook the food to enjoy the surroundings, this is certainly not the case here. But neither does one have to overlook the surroundings. The Green Tree is located next door to The Old Original Clothes Horse, a dress shop/boutique that was Mrs. McVay's first business venture here. The structure that houses both enterprises probably dates from the middle of the eighteenth century. Inside, the cherrywood paneled pub has rough pine furniture and a huge fireplace. The larger dining room is a bit more formal, with parquet floors and high ceilings. Seasonal events and entertainment are available. In 1975 they had a Polish Christmas celebration and, occasionally, eighteenth-century strains of lutes, zithers, and recorders played by musicians in period garb drift through the conversation.

Everything on the menu is worth ordering. The Hampton crab, roast duckling, and the Old Alexandria ham loaf are especially good, as are any of the homemade soups, breads, and pastries.

The menu is as fun to read as it is to order from. Mrs. McVay, relying on her time spent as a copywriter with an ad firm, has written a menu that is as funny as it is historically accurate. For instance, the selection of the Hampton crab begins: "We follow a recipe that was used in 1789 for Hampton Crab. The original directions began, 'Send William out for 24 Prime Crabs.' We had to skip that part because we didn't have anyone named William to send. But save for the lack of a William. . . ."

One other helpful feature of the menu is a recommended selection of wines for each entrée, an excellent collection of imported wines ranging from $4.95 to $14.50 per bottle.

And the prices, though not quite eighteenth century, have not caught up with this half of the twentieth century. The entrées range from a low of $5.95 for the broiled trout to a high of $9.95 for an enormous steak.

THE INN
PURCELLVILLE, VA.

He looks so much like the Colonel Sanders of chicken fame that he'd be a walking trademark infringement if he sold the fried fowl. But Colonel Bertram and his wife, Irene, owners of The Inn in Purcellville, serve chicken in more sophisticated ways than Bertram's lookalike. Unlike many country inns, this one has a French flavor, and fried chicken is nowhere on the menu.

The turn-of-the-century farmhouse sits comfortably amid a grove of cooling trees, and overlooks the rolling hills and fairways of a golf course.

The Colonel, as he is known (U.S. Army retired), was a breeder of black Angus cattle in New England when he met his French-born wife, who was the proprietor of the Egremont Tavern in Massachusetts. They moved south and opened up The Inn for Thanksgiving in 1968. Since then, it has become a favorite with Washington area residents, and for some D.C. families driving to Purcellville has become a family tradition for Sunday dinner.

Diners enter The Inn through the small stone-walled basement tavern, which has the look and homey feel of an old-time ordinary. This is the casual side of The Inn

ADDRESS: Route 7 on the eastern edge of Purcellville, Virginia 22132

TELEPHONE: 703-338-6088

FACILITIES: Dining only; daily from noon to 2:30 p.m. and from 6 to 8:30 p.m., Sundays and holidays from noon to 8 p.m.

RESERVATIONS: Recommended

DRESS: Nice casual to informal

CREDIT CARDS: American Express, BankAmericard, Master Charge

and, due to my aversion to formality, my favorite.

The second floor of dining overlooks the golf course and is a more formal dining area. But regardless of where you sit, the service is friendly; in fact, we were smothered in service, being waited on at various times by our waitress, two or three other bus people, stewards, and assistants, all of whom had warm personalities.

The meal started with a small, hot loaf of homemade bread. The little loaves were a prelude to a meal that was prepared with care. The French onion soup was thick with onion and cheese, and the entrées and vegetables were outstanding. The baked shrimp stuffed with crabmeat was as good as anything I have had on the Eastern Shore, as were the sautéed langostinos in a mild garlic butter. The vegetables were fresh and delicately seasoned. The sole disappointment of the meal was dessert, and what a disappointment. I ordered a slice of strawberry-rhubarb pie and got a slice of store-bought pie. When you order dessert here, ask if the dish is homemade. Otherwise, it is not worth the calories. Dinner for two cost $29.

L'AUBERGE
MIDDLEBURG, VA.

Inns are for making friends. At least the potential is there—people go to inns with more in mind than just eating, and when food is not their only object they tend to take time to enjoy the surroundings and the people.

So it was at L'Auberge. The cozy little room with its six tables, massive French armoire, and rustling fire contained one person when we arrived, a young man who sat facing our table as he sampled a bottle of red Bordeaux. He greeted us and before we knew it, we were caught in a delightful conversation that lasted the entire meal. Rusty Fowler—president of a rock music management company, friendly chap from Market, Virginia, able fire tender, genial conversationalist, friend of the chef—was a pleasure to meet.

It's amazing how many times we have driven through the town of Middleburg without noticing L'Auberge. Did we really miss it all of those times or did it just appear from the Twilight Zone? No matter; we found it and had one of those experiences that left us with a good feeling.

The massive house, built circa 1804, is a brick two-story structure with Georgian outlines and a two-story front porch in the style of southern plantation homes.

ADDRESS: Route 50, Middleburg, Virginia 22117
TELEPHONE: 703-687-6139
FACILITIES: Dining only; Thursdays through Mondays from
11:30 a.m. to 3 p.m. and from 5:30 to 9:30 p.m. Closed Tuesdays
and Wednesdays
RESERVATIONS: Recommended
DRESS: Nice casual to informal
CREDIT CARDS: BankAmericard, personal checks

Shuttered windows, a wrought-iron Victorian fence, and
latticework porch railings all make this building remarkable.

We entered the high-ceilinged anteroom/reception
area that was furnished with period antiques. We noticed
a garden-type room to the left with bright green and
silver latticework wallpaper, and were then ushered to
our table by the oak-manteled fireplace. The French armoire behind us was massive, beautifully restored, and
outfitted with gleaming brass hinges and brass ornamental work with hammered designs.

The service was friendly and ever so correct without being stuffy. According to Rusty, who eats here often,
L'Auberge is a favorite eating spot for local celebrities:
Liz Taylor is reputed to frequent it as are many of the
wealthy Middleburg horse and plantation owners.

We started the meal with a slightly spicy shrimp
bisque. It's likely that no one in the world makes bisque
better. We then had our main course: Shan had duck and
I had the Bas Pernod—striped bass flamed with Pernod.
Both were out of this world.

The duck was crisp on the outside and was not fatty
or greasy. It was de-boned with only two main bones
remaining and was glazed with honey and lemon. The
anise-licorice flavor of the pernod was an unusual one
to sample with fish and was very good.

We finished with chocolate mousse—very rich and
light—and coffee. L'Auberge serves a house coffee, with
a bit of espresso mixed in, that is heavenly and by far
the best of any restaurant we have ever been to. Dinner
for two was $33.

The reasons for the excellent food are the inn's two
chefs, Sarah Dodderidge and Steve Jaeger. Although it
really should not be so, it is rare to find a woman chef.
Women are expected to cook at home but are discrim-

inated against when they want to cook in a restaurant.
The fact that the restaurant is owned by a woman, Sally
Guthrie, could have something to do with its raised con-
sciousness.

Sarah studied and was accredited as a chef in Edin-
burgh, Scotland ("they have a close connection with the
French," she told us) and studied under the ex-chef of
the Dorchester. Her specialties are fish and poultry. Steve
Jaeger, on the other hand, specializes in the inn's red
meat dishes. Jaeger was accredited as a chef after study
at the Culinary Institute of America in New York City.

As you would expect from their training, the menu
is more French than old colony Virginia. Lapin au
Moutard (sautéed rabbit), Tournedos Chorson, and es-
calopes de veau creme au champignons are some of the
main dishes, which are all very good.

L'AUBERGE CHEZ FRANÇOIS
GREAT FALLS, VA.

In France, lovers of fine food frequently take to the small back roads of the countryside in search of les auberges, tiny inns offering a cozy setting and fine meals that are usually prepared by the chef/owner and other members of his family. Nowhere is the tradition of l'auberge greater than in the green province of Alsace. In early 1976, after twenty-six years of operating one of the finest restaurants in Washington, D.C., François Haeringer and his family moved to Great Falls, Virginia, and opened an Alsatian auberge. Both the atmosphere and the food at L'Auberge Chez François are perfect.

The inn is located in the midst of beautiful, rolling countryside. Although the outside of the building is not exceptional, the inside is very cozy and cheery, with a huge freestanding brick fireplace.

We started the evening with appetizers. Shan ordered quiche and I ordered the soup d'jour, *potage parmentier*. The quiche had a flaky crust and a custardy and light filling. My soup was a hot version of vichyssoise.

For an entrée, I ordered sautéed scallops in a light Provençal sauce. It was done to perfection. Shan ordered one of the day's specialties, a fresh salmon soufflé that would make a salmon hater ask for seconds.

The menu changes each day according to what foods

ADDRESS: Springvale Road, Great Falls, Virginia 22066.
Take the Beltway (I-495) to Route 193, Georgetown Pike.
About a mile past Great Falls, turn right on Springvale Road
and go about two miles. Coming from the other direction, take
Route 7 to Springvale Road, go north to the inn
TELEPHONE: 703-759-3800
FACILITIES: Dining only; Tuesday through Friday from
11:30 a.m. to 2 p.m. and 6 to 9 p.m., Saturday 6 to 9 p.m.,
Sunday 4 to 8 p.m.
RESERVATIONS: Required
DRESS: Informal
CREDIT CARDS: American Express, BankAmericard, Carte
Blanche, Diner's Club, Master Charge

can be obtained fresh. There's simply no room for canned
or frozen food in this kitchen.

Entrées were followed by a green salad of endive
and romaine lettuce, with a dressing that had a heavy
garlic accent. We then finished the meal with a couple of
exceptional desserts—white mousse and raspberry tart.
The raspberries were fresh, even though it was late October. My white mousse contained a hint of raspberry and
was topped with a bit of kirsch, fresh whipped cream,
and a fresh strawberry. The coffee, too, was exceptional.
Our dinner for two cost $35.

After eating we introduced ourselves to François
Haeringer and listened to him speak of his love for his
art.

"But come, let me show you my kitchen," he said
urging us through the swinging doors and into the gleaming inner sanctum that bustled with activity. In the
middle of it all was a calm figure in white orchestrating
the activity. "This is my chef," François proudly told
us. "My son Jacques."

We toured the pastry area, where all of the inn's
bread and pastry is made, and then the meat section,
where François personally carves every cut of meat used
to insure that it is perfectly cut and proportioned.

Reservations should be made far in advance. "I am
having these troubles," Mr. Haeringer lamented. "I only
have so many tables and there are people who are being
turned away." I suggested that this was a good problem
to have. "Non, because they are getting mad at me. They
don't understand."

Understand and make your reservations in advance.

LAUREL BRIGADE
LEESBURG, VA.

There seems to be a word missing from Roy Flippo's dictionary — inflation. As we settled our bill the morning after staying at Flippo's establishment, the Laurel Brigade in Leesburg, I was agog to find that the room rates are only a dollar more than they were when Flippo's parents reopened the inn in 1947. We paid $9. Nine dollars? I asked if he had added things up correctly. Nine dollars; six for a single room.

The tariff for the room was really the only surprise about the Laurel Brigade, since we had gone there expecting the friendly service and the good meal in historic surroundings that we received. The menu covers a wide range, from the typical country dishes of fried chicken, steaks, and ham to such entrées as crab imperial and broiled flounder stuffed with backfin crabmeat. We savored the flounder and crabmeat and enjoyed the vegetables that accompanied the meal. We had fresh squash, lima beans, and an oven-broiled potato.

The summer squash was buttery and smooth. "I brought it in from my garden this afternoon," our waitress informed us.

The dinner was crowned with fresh peach shortcake. Dinner for two cost $20.

The rooms are modestly furnished with a collection

ADDRESS: On Route 7 just west of the intersection of Route 15 in Leesburg, Virginia 22075
TELEPHONE: 703-777-1010
FACILITIES: Six rooms; dining daily from noon to 2 p.m. and from 5 to 8 p.m.
RATES: $6 a night for a single, $9 for a double room
RESERVATIONS: Required for lodging, recommended for meals
DRESS: Nice casual to informal
CREDIT CARDS: None

of antiques mixed with some not-very-attractive modern pieces and accessories. The rooms look as if they have not been redecorated since the inn's reopening in 1947. However, for $9 per night, they are a great bargain. The most attractive feature of the rooms is the wide-planked pine floors.

Although various parts of the Laurel Brigade have been added over the years, its first section dates back to 1766. The house had been used as an inn, an attorney's office, and a private residence prior to 1817, when it was bought by Eleanor and Hendry Peers and converted back to its original use under the name of the Peers Hotel.

The hotel had a very good reputation, and according to early records, prominent landowners met there regularly to discuss business. Its reputation was such that, in 1825, the Marquis de Lafayette, President John Adams, and ex-President James Monroe stopped there to eat while on their way to Monroe's estate at Oak Hill.

The hotel closed after Mrs. Peers' death in 1835 and was a private residence until 1947, when Roy Flippo, Sr., bought it and turned it into an inn once again. Today, the inn is run by Roy, Jr., and his wife, Ellen.

The inn was named after a daring and renowned Confederate cavalry group called the Laurel Brigade, which drew many of its members, including its commander, from the Leesburg area.

The last cavalry charge of the Civil War was made by the Laurel Brigade a short distance from the Appomattox Courthouse. The brigade never surrendered but rode off after the battle to Lynchburg, where it disbanded.

OLD CLUB
ALEXANDRIA, VA.

The night was cold enough to freeze light in its tracks; the wind probed and pierced through our coats in the insidious way that wind can. All of the clichés having to do with well diggers, brass monkeys, and witches were borne out.

But an oasis awaited us at the Old Club in Alexandria, where we received a warm blast of air and a cheery welcome as we entered its portals. The dark glowing grains of wood paneling added to the warmth of the radiating fire. And the low ceilings gave the place an air of intimacy and relaxation.

As we walked in the Washington Street entrance, our attention was captured by a small restored room to the right of the reception hall, a room furnished with memorabilia and antiques relating to the life and times of George Washington. George and Martha Washington would undoubtedly approve of the dignified manner in which their portraits gaze across this restored eighteenth-century room at guests. Although, George might not consider it appropriate for Martha's picture to be here at all, since this was the clubhouse where he went to relax over a few ales with his cronies.

The clubhouse was originally down the hill along the Potomac, but was moved to its present site about

ADDRESS: 555 S. Washington Street, Alexandria, Virginia 23314

TELEPHONE: 703-549-4555

FACILITIES: Dining only; Tuesday through Friday from 11:30 a.m. to 3 p.m., Saturdays until 9:45 p.m., Sundays from noon to 8:45 p.m. Closed Mondays and Christmas Day

RESERVATIONS: Required on weekends, recommended at all times

DRESS: Nice casual for lunch, informal at dinner

CREDIT CARDS: American Express, BankAmericard, and Master Charge

1790. Among the other revolutionary luminaries who were members of the club was George Mason, the author of the Bill of Rights.

The small restored room is the only original part of the present-day Old Club. It is roped off and separate from the dining rooms, but can be easily examined at length from the visitor's section by the reception room.

All the seafood dishes served in the dining rooms are painstakingly well prepared and delicious. But a special treat is what the menu calls ''A Real Southern Dinner.'' You can satisfy your Southern food cravings with peanut butter soup, followed by baked country ham and accompanied by cornbread, blackeyed peas, candied sweet potatoes, and a slice of pecan pie that would make a die-hard Yankee believe in Confederate war bonds.

RED FOX INN
MIDDLEBURG, VA.

Snowflakes swirled across Virginia's Route 50 as we headed northwest from Washington toward Middleburg. It was a gray, cold winter day—the sort of day that normally brought wishful thoughts of the Caribbean. But today, we had another warm haven in mind: the Red Fox Inn in Middleburg.

As I entered through the broad oaken front door, the cold dissolved in the warmth of the fireplaces, whitewashed stone walls, broad-beamed ceilings, and a friendly atmosphere that by itself could have warmed up the weather.

We had come with another couple and were seated in the tavern, next to a fire fueled with pine knots and chunks of split oak.

While the United States was celebrating its Bicentennial, the Red Fox Inn was getting ready for its 250th anniversary. It was established in 1728 and is the second oldest continuously operating inn in America. It is a favorite with the horse set and with those who come to watch the equestrian events for which this area of Virginia is known. To most Americans riding in a fox hunt is a bit of landed gentry esoterica that lives on in the movies or in the lives of very few of the idle rich. But in

ADDRESS: Route 50, Middleburg, Virginia 22117
TELEPHONE: 703-687-6301
FACILITIES: Six rooms in the inn, two-level guest house; dining Monday through Saturday from 8 a.m. to 9 p.m., Sundays until 8 p.m.
RATES: From $18 for a single with semi-private bath to $55 for a two-person suite
RESERVATIONS: Recommended
DRESS: Informal in the day, formal at night
CREDIT CARDS: BankAmericard and Master Charge

Middleburg this and other equestrian events are an integral part of the lifestyle and the economy.

Middleburg was a favorite with the Kennedy family when JFK was President, and the first family frequently visited it for church on Sundays. The Middleburg Training Track, founded by Mr. Paul Mellon; the Foxcroft School; the National Beagle Trials; Upperville Horse Show; and many annual hunts are near the inn.

The main reason for visiting the inn is to see its well-restored dining areas and lodgings, and the colonial and other antique furniture.

The food, though adequate, does not begin to measure up to the setting. Many of the seafood dishes taste as if prepared from pre-packaged frozen concoctions, and other main dishes don't seem to fare much better. The one exceptional thing on the menu is the German chocolate cake, which is too wonderful to describe. Dinner for two cost $25.

Although the food is only adequate, the Red Fox Inn has remained one of our favorite places, which we've visited many times primarily for the pleasant dining experience. The lovely setting and the good and friendly service make a visit worthwhile.

A good time to visit the inn is for a late breakfast on Sundays. They have no special brunch menu, but if you get there early, you'll have the inn to yourself to enjoy the setting and to examine the old pewter and copper furnishings hung on the walls. Make reservations and request the tavern.

MAINLAND MARYLAND

Maryland is like a miniature United States, with a greater diversity of geography, people, and customs than is usually found within one state. There's a piece of it out west in the mountains that's like its neighboring West Virginia. Here, two boundaries of Maryland —the Potomac River and the Mason-Dixon line—come within a few miles of each other and threaten to completely cut off that section from the rest of the state. The eastern shore, with its maritime traditions, is like another country entirely.

The central portion of Maryland, which we're calling "Mainland Maryland," is a region that has always suffered from a sort of cultural and geographic schizophrenia—it was a border state in the Civil War and its citizens were bitterly divided on the slavery issue. Today, it still doesn't know which side it belongs to. Its manners are generally southern, yet it has a northern political orientation. It seems very rural—until you get to Baltimore or the Maryland suburbs of Washington.

The Appalachian Mountains in the western portion of this section form the backdrop for Cunningham Falls State Park and the adjoining Catoctin Mountain National Park, which is the site of the presidential retreat of Camp David. The parks provide plenty of activities for the hiker-outdoorsperson, but about all the unathletic visitor can do is stare through the brush around the presidential hideaway and snap photos of family members standing by the sign to the entrance (although there is a crafts and folklore festival in May).

Paralleling the Potomac River—the southern boundary of the state—is the longest, narrowest national park in the world, the Chesapeake and Ohio Canal National Park, which runs 185 miles from the Georgetown section of Washington, D.C., to Cumberland, Maryland. The canal was conceived by George Washington, and some of the early work on it was done under his direction. Today, the hiking-biking trail, which was once the towpath for mules pulling barges, is a delight for the afternoon daytripper or for the adventurous soul who wants to travel the entire length.

One stop off the canal, near Sharpsburg, is the National Historical Park of Antietam, site of the bloodiest battle of the Civil War. Further along and a bit north is Sugarloaf Mountain and the Stronghold mansion, which make for very interesting sightseeing. Also close by is the small hamlet of Lilypons, with 1,800 acres of exotic water plants.

Traveling more inland, we come to New Market, which is a jam-packed collection of antique stores and friendly people. Still further north is the farming country of Carroll County and the Carroll County Farm Museum. (If you like museums, another unique one is the National Capital Trolley Museum in the Washington suburb of Wheaton, Maryland.)

Just a short drive from Carroll County is the horse-and-mansion country outside Baltimore, which is straight out of the book of dreams. Mansions and estates jam the countryside, and anyone without a tree-lined driveway four miles long is a pauper—relatively speaking. The Vanderbilt horse farm, which has produced greats like Man O'War, is located on Reisterstown Road between Hunt Valley and Reisterstown. Horse racing, as one gathers from the farms, is big fun in Maryland.

BLAIR MANSION INN
SILVER SPRING, MD.

Well, it *used* to be in the country. The old Victorian mansion that houses the Blair Mansion Inn was built about 1890 and was in the middle of the Maryland countryside when it was finished. Today, the Blair Mansion Inn is a small enclave of calm amid the bustle of traffic that streams by its location on Eastern Avenue, just across the District of Columbia line. But when you step through the entryway into the darkened vestibule with its massive antique hall tree, you can forget the commotion outside and imagine being returned to the era when the roads in front were still country lanes.

According to the inn's brochure, the Blair Mansion Inn was built on a portion of the Pierce-Shoemaker Estate, which was originally granted to George Pierce in 1685 by King Charles II of England.

In 1959 Blair Mansion Inn was extensively renovated and the semicircular Terrace Room was added. This represents the only structural change in the old mansion other than the addition of an efficient and modern kitchen. The building has eleven fireplaces, of which seven are still operational, and has the distinction of being the first home in the area to have indoor plumbing.

In the foyer and throughout the various dining rooms are many antiques of exceptional interest. The magnifi-

ADDRESS: 7711 Eastern Avenue, N.W., Silver Spring, Maryland 20910

TELEPHONE: 301-588-1688

FACILITIES: Dining only; Tuesday through Thursday from 11:30 a.m. to 10 p.m., until 11 p.m. Fridays, noon to 11 p.m. Saturdays, noon to 9 p.m. Sundays

RESERVATIONS: Recommended

DRESS: Informal

CREDIT CARDS: American Express, BankAmericard, Diner's Club, Master Charge

cent James & Bolmstorn piano, located in the main foyer, stood in the White House during Woodrow Wilson's Administration. When the White House was remodeled during Truman's first term, this fine instrument was acquired by Blair Mansion Inn for their collection.

Another item of great interest is the grandfather's clock, also located in the main foyer. This clock won the grand prize at the 1915 Panama Pacific International Exposition. One of the most entertaining relics is a genuine nickelodeon. It was built in 1910 by Seeburg and is one of the first jukeboxes in this country.

The seven dining rooms are scattered throughout the house and decorated rather eclectically, with one room resembling an old-style ordinary and another the epitome of a formal Victorian dining room.

The diner fares best when sticking to the traditional Maryland dishes that the inn has become known for: Chesapeake Bay seafood, roast duck, chicken, and turkey. The crab imperial has long been a favorite.

The homemade desserts are, in my estimation, their strong point, with such dishes as apple brown Betty, homemade pecan pie, and strawberry shortcake. Dinner for two cost $30.

The Blair Mansion Inn is the perfect lunchtime retreat from the manic pace of modern life. Several people have told me that they felt the standards of cooking and cleanliness have declined in the past few years, but on two recent occasions I found the food well prepared and the waitress and hostess friendly. Its closeness to Washington is its main advantage over the other inns.

BROOK FARM INN
CHEVY CHASE, MD.

The strains of a Strauss waltz wafted through the high-ceilinged dining room, capturing the diner's attention and silencing the clink of glass and silverware. When it was over, the pianist rose for the well-deserved applause.

The guests at the Brook Farm Inn returned to their *sauerbraten, schnitzel,* and *choucroute.* We love middle European food and this, according to our friends who have been through Germany and Austria, was as good as the food eaten there. Without being able to make that kind of comparison, I could still appreciate the quality of the food.

I had the *choucroute* (porkchop, bratwurst, and sauerkraut), sweet and sour red cabbage, and a stein of frosty Bavarian lager. The *choucroute, wiener schnitzel,* the roast duck with apricot ginger sauce, and the *sauerbraten* and potato pancakes are all classic dishes beautifully prepared.

Apple strudel or walnut cake should be ordered even if you don't ordinarily eat dessert. Dinner for two cost $25.

Brook Farm's proprietor and chef, Wolfgang Erbe, is as interesting as the food he prepares. Originally from Germany, he has had restaurants in Switzerland, Ger-

ADDRESS: 7101 Brookville Road, Chevy Chase, Maryland 20015. It is easily accessible from the Beltway (I-495) Exit 20
TELEPHONE: 301-652-8820
FACILITIES: Dining only; Tuesday through Sunday from 5 to 10 p.m.
RESERVATIONS: Recommended
DRESS: Informal
CREDIT CARDS: American Express, Carte Blanche, Diner's Club

many, Brazil, and the United States. The flags of every country in which he has been a restaurateur fly from the balcony of the dining room. Erbe was associated with Sardi's in New York before coming to Washington. His wife, Christa, is the hostess at Brook Farm.

The interior of Brook Farm—with the mounted stag's head over the massive stone fireplace flanked with antique flintlock rifles, the varnished knotty pine walls, and the high ceilings with dark stained beams—makes you expect to see hunters in *lederhosen* and hiking boots come stomping through the front door.

Brook Farm was once an elegant Maryland country estate and the site of many elegant teas held for Eleanor Roosevelt when FDR was President. Although suburban Washington has grown up around it, it still retains a country-like air, being surrounded by trees and elegant homes, and being somewhat off the beaten path.

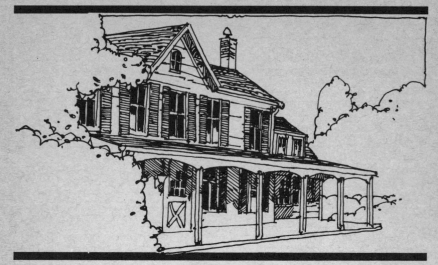

COMUS INN
COMUS, MD.

The day had dawned crisp and blue. The woods had that slightly greenish tinge painted over the grays and browns of its winter armor, and the fact that you couldn't see through the trees quite as far as the week before held the promise that spring would return soon.

It was a picnic type of day as we entered the gates of Stronghold on Sugarloaf Mountain and threaded our way up the mountain road. Finally, we reached a spot to leave the car and hiked along the trails to the top of the mountain, which has a commanding view of the Maryland and Virginia countryside. Indeed, it was for this vantage point, which offered the perfect reconnaissance position, that Union and Confederate troops fought fiercely.

The summit of Sugarloaf that was so important to the combatants in the Civil War was once owned by William Corcoran, the distinguished American who endowed the Corcoran Art Museum and School in Washington, D.C.

The mountain was discovered by the late Gordon Strong about the turn of this century while on a bicycle trip from Washington. He acquired the mountain bit by bit over the years, and then built on it a massive and beautiful Georgian-style mansion, which still stands. He

ADDRESS: Route 109, Comus, Maryland 20753. Take I-270 north from the Beltway (I-495) about 22 miles to Route 109. Take 109 west to its junction with Route 95
TELEPHONE: 301-428-8593
FACILITIES: Dining only; Sunday through Thursday from noon to 9 p.m., Friday and Saturday until 11 p.m.
RESERVATIONS: Recommended
DRESS: Casual for lunch, informal all other times
CREDIT CARDS: American Express, BankAmericard

called his home and the land around it "Stronghold."

Stronghold is a 3,000-acre, privately owned preserve that is administered by a nonprofit corporation that Strong formed in 1946. Although the mansion is not open to the public, visitors are welcome to enjoy the views from the Sugarloaf summit during daylight hours, seven days a week.

One of the sights from Sugarloaf Mountain is the Comus Inn, located at the base of the mountain. George Washington never stayed at the inn, but he did visit the town of Comus in 1770 and was impressed by the mountain, the green valley, and the rolling meadows. The Comus Inn is located on one of two parcels of land once owned by Washington.

The inn was built of huge hand-hewn logs and timbers in 1860, although it has been added to and renovated in the past century. Its long shaded front porch, gabled roof, and shuttered windows make this an inviting place in any season. An antique store is located in an adjacent building.

The interior of the Comus Inn is mostly undistinguished, but the rooms at the rear on the glassed-in porch are lovely, since they give a clear view of Sugarloaf Mountain.

Dining here begins with an elaborate relish and salad bar stuffed with all manner of country delicacies—apple butter, watermelon pickles, chow-chow, corn relish, cole slaw, and all kinds of salad fixings. The homemade soups are hearty and tasty. Entrées are country staples: ham, chicken, steaks, and broiled fish. All of them are enjoyable and prepared simply, rather as they might be in the cook's own kitchen at home. A meal for two cost about $12.

There is live music and dancing on weekends until 1 a.m.

MAUDE'S
OWINGS MILLS, MD.

Samuel Owings' huge estate house was built in 1767, just upstream from his mills (for which the town was named). It is a beautifully preserved example of colonial architecture, with classic chimneys at each end and extra wide doors with eared moldings. The mills are gone today and Owings' home is now an inn serving food good enough to travel a distance for. A name change from Samuel Owings, 1767, to its present one of Maude's is the only thing that disappointed us here.

For fine dining there are two rooms at Maude's, Le Petit Gourmet and La Dolce Vita. As the names suggest, the first room serves French food, and the second serves Italian (the French menu is available only in Le Petit Gourmet, the Italian menu only in La Dolce Vita). There is a more casual sandwich dining room called the Bicycle Shop, which is open for lunch.

The choice of which room to try was a hard one, since we like both types of food. We solved it very scientifically by flipping a coin, and chose Le Petit Gourmet. By the way, when you make your reservation you should specify which room you want.

Our dining room was furnished in an early American, federal style. Queen Anne chairs were set among the

ADDRESS: Owings Mills, Maryland 21117. Take the Reisterstown Road (Route 140) Exit from the Baltimore Beltway (I-695); go about three miles to Painters Mill Road and turn left. Maude's will be on your left in about ¼ mile, at the corner of Dolfield Road

TELEPHONE: 301-363-3676

FACILITIES: Dining only; daily from 11 a.m. to 10 p.m. (The Bicycle Shop is open from 11 a.m. to 2 p.m.)

RESERVATIONS: Required

DRESS: Informal

CREDIT CARDS: American Express, BankAmericard, Master Charge

wainscotting and decorative moldings, and there were wide-planked floors and a fireplace that, unfortunately, had no fire in it the night we visited.

We started with hot muffins and bread delivered before we even ordered by an assistant waiter in breeches and kneesocks. Next came a relish-dip with raw vegetables and a blue cheese sauce. The dish was stacked high with sliced carrots, celery, radishes, cucumbers, freshly sliced mushrooms, and hot pickled peppers.

When it came time to order we both opted for lobster bisque. Then I ordered the seafood crêpes and Shan ordered the fresh mushrooms stuffed with crabmeat. Neither was a mistake. My crêpes were light and thin and the filling was wonderful. Fresh scallops, crabmeat, and mushrooms were sautéed in butter with shallots, with chablis and pernod, and finished with cream. The crêpes were then topped with a Mornay sauce. The mushrooms were filled with crabmeat and sautéed mushrooms in a cream sauce and were topped with the same Mornay sauce.

We followed that with a fresh spinach salad topped with sliced mushrooms.

Shan ordered cherries jubilee for dessert, which took the small dining room by storm. This is not the dessert for people who don't want to have the attention of everyone in the room on them. Carl, our waiter, wheeled out a cart and put on a flashy show by pouring flaming brandy back and forth between two goblets, a feat that won him a round of applause when he finally poured the brandy into the skillet with the cherries. The cherries were delicious, although eating them was an anticlimax. Dinner for two cost $39.

MEADOWLARK INN
POOLESVILLE, MD.

Take a century-old farm-house, turn every room into a dining room, add an owner-chef whose food reflects the fact that he enjoys cooking, subtract all but the most friendly hostesses and waitresses, and divide the price into half what the patron expects. This is the formula that has made the Meadowlark Inn in Poolesville, Maryland, so popular with area residents.

We came early for Sunday dinner and were seated on the front porch, which is now enclosed. We looked through the grove of shady maple trees at the sleepy country town. In addition to the porch, you can dine in a very formal Victorian motif dining room, suitably wallpapered and dimly lit, and a brick dining room with a fireplace that is ideal for warming up on a cold winter night.

The meal started with a relish dish, piled high with crisp sliced raw vegetables and an ice-cream scoop of cheese spread that was mild like cheddar but with an edge from a bit of horseradish. We enjoyed it with the vegetables and with crackers. The homemade salad dressing had an unusual and elusive taste.

The Meadowlark Inn takes great pains with their pre-entrée courses. My vegetable soup was homemade, thick with barley and with so many vegetable chunks

ADDRESS: Route 107, Poolesville, Maryland 20837. Take Route 28 to Beallsville; turn west onto Route 109 to Poolesville. Then turn left on Route 107; the inn will be less than a half mile on your left

TELEPHONE: 301-428-8937

FACILITIES: Dining only; lunch served (from buffet or menu) Tuesday through Saturday 11:30 a.m. to 2:30 p.m., dinner Tuesday through Saturday from 5 to 9:45 p.m., Sunday from noon to 9 p.m.

RESERVATIONS: Recommended

DRESS: Nice casual to informal

CREDIT CARDS: None

that it was almost a meatless stew. The fruit cups showed the same care—chunks of fresh canteloupe, orange slices, some fermented pineapple that tasted like it had been taken from a rum *topf,* and a scoop of sherbet.

The entrées are prepared just as well, from the manicotti to the lamb with mint jelly.

Meals come as a complete dinner that includes appetizer, salad, entrée, dessert, and beverage. They range from $5.95 for the manicotti to $9.95 for a huge sixteen-ounce steak. Other entrées include crab imperial, baked stuffed filet of sole, broiled salmon steak, veal parmigiana, and barbecued prime ribs. Quite a selection for such a small inn.

Although the inn has been in operation since 1970, the present owners, Trudy and Michael Zirpolo, just started operating it in early 1974. Since then, the inn's reputation has steadily grown.

MEALY'S HOTEL
NEW MARKET, MD.

Once you get past the exterior, which is a perfect example of the American malady of not leaving a good thing alone, Mealy's Hotel in New Market is a pleasant place to eat. To enlarge its interior space by about five feet by forty feet, white painted aluminum panels, storm doors, and aluminum sash storm windows have been added to the front of this beautiful three-story Georgian brick structure, which is 176 years old.

But fortunately, the bad impression made by the defacing of the exterior is soon dissolved by the classic country dining and warm atmosphere within. A relish table with fresh tomatoes, cole slaw, cottage cheese, and apple butter made with a touch of honey is a perfect start to the meal. This is followed by cheese and crackers, and a salad.

The seafood is delicately prepared. We especially enjoyed the vegetables accompanying the meal—bread dough fritters, southern-style green beans cooked with ham, and creamy scalloped potatoes. Unfortunately, many of the desserts—especially the pies—are store-bought and are not worth trying.

Mealy's Hotel, which has served New Market since about 1800, provided overnight lodging until the mid-1940's. The main dining room is a low-ceilinged room

ADDRESS: Main Street, New Market, Maryland 21774. Follow
I-70 to Route 144, about 10 miles east of Frederick
TELEPHONE: 301-865-5488
FACILITIES: Dining only; lunch served Tuesday through
Friday noon to 3 p.m., Saturday until 3:30 p.m.; Dinner served
Tuesday through Saturday from 3:30 to 8:30 p.m., Sundays from
noon to 8:30 p.m.
RESERVATIONS: Not required
DRESS: Casual to informal
CREDIT CARDS: American Express, BankAmericard

lit with old oil lamps that have been converted to elec-
tricity. The wide-planked floors of the rooms above can
be seen running across the exposed ceiling beams.

The two plaster walls on the dining room ends serve
to counterpoint the one paneled wall and the brick wall.
Even though the room is quite large, it manages to be
cozy. The parents of the present owner, Dick Mealy,
bought the hotel in 1918. Mealy's wife, Frances, now
takes the day-to-day responsibility of management. Mrs.
Mealy often treats her customers to a boisterous display
as she swirls around the dining room, through the reception areas, and back into the kitchen dressed in fuzzy
bedroom slippers and a kimono.

The town of New Market is an antique hunter's
wonderland, with just about every building housing a
shop of some sort. There are more than forty such stores
in this tiny place that was once a booming pioneer town
along the National Pike. Main Street, which once had
eight hotels and taverns, saw steady streams of Conestoga
wagons headed west toward Ohio and herds of livestock
being driven east to the Baltimore markets.

In addition to antique shops, there is a flower and
basket shop, a shop selling candles and soap, a Scottish
import shop, the Thistle Stop (Gaelic spoken here), a
silver shop, an old book and prints shop, and The Strawberry Inn, which is a great place to spend the night (see
page 176).

Aside from the concentration of antique shops, the
most remarkable thing about New Market is how friendly
everyone is. We admired the unusual red and white
geraniums in the window box outside the Pine Shop, and
its proprietor, Mrs. Louise Bennett, insisted on giving
us a cutting, which now graces our living room.

MILTON INN
SPARKS, MD.

Thirty years before the American Revolution began, the Milton Inn was built to provide the drivers of devout Quakers a place to rest while their employers met for religious services at the New Gunpowder Meeting House about a mile and a half away. It remains today as the oldest building in Baltimore city and county.

It was used as an inn until 1847, when it was converted into a classical school for the sons of prominent Maryland families, one of whom was John Wilkes Booth, assassin of President Lincoln. The school became a private residence in 1895 and remained as such until 1947 when it was once again restored to its original purpose as an inn.

John Emerson Lamb, who founded the school, named it for John Milton, author of *Paradise Lost*. The Milton Inn is almost paradise regained, with a menu so long that it must have been written by James Michener, and a wine cellar that would almost put the Chateau Rothschild to shame. In case your waiter doesn't make the offer, ask to go to the wine cellar to pick out your own bottle; that is the house policy, but not all of the waiters remember to mention it.

An evening here begins with before-dinner libations taken in the comfortable sitting room with its roaring

ADDRESS: Route 45 (York Road), Sparks, Maryland 21152.
It's about 17 miles north of Baltimore. Take I-83, the Shawan
Road Exit toward Hunt Valley. Drive past the Hunt Valley Inn,
past one light to a stop sign where the road deadends into
Route 45. Turn left; the Milton Inn will be on your right in
about three miles
TELEPHONE: 301-771-4366
FACILITIES: Dining only; Tuesday through Sunday from
11:30 a.m. to 2:30 p.m., 6 p.m. to midnight
RESERVATIONS: Required
DRESS: Informal, men must wear jackets
CREDIT CARDS: American Express, BankAmericard, Master
Charge

fire. The room is appropriately dark and cozy. However,
this coziness makes it a perfect target for tobacco smoke,
and we passed up a drink there for one at our table. The
management is sensitive, and if smoke bothers you, you
can be seated at your table instead.

The smell of the hickory fire permeates the entire
inn, and you get the feeling of the hearth even in the other
rooms. There are three dining rooms: two rather large
ones and a smaller one with about eight two-person tables.
This room is the most romantic we have ever dined in,
and is definitely our favorite of the three rooms.

The interior of the inn is right in keeping with the
inn's rough fieldstone exterior, gabled roof, and ivy-
covered walls. The entrance leads into a pub; from there
you can go to either the formally decorated Federal style
dining rooms or to the more rustic colonial room that has
settings for couples only.

The food is very good, although the meals suffer
from poor service. The waits between courses were almost interminable, and a Caesar salad, which should
have been prepared fresh at our table, had obviously
been made some time before and arrived soggy and
wilted. We sent it back and they were gracious about it.

We started with soup. I ordered onion, Shan ordered
turtle. The onion soup was only fair, but the clear turtle
soup was much better. Shan ordered lobster stuffed with
crabmeat and I ordered a baked seafood platter contain-
ing lobster, shrimp, crab imperial, and frog legs. There
was a lot of shell in the crab, both in my platter and in
Shan's stuffing. The entrées were not very hot when they
arrived and the lobster needed, and lacked, some melted

butter.

Dessert was a great improvement. My French straw-berry cake arrived with fresh strawberries. The three delicate layers tasted as if they had been soaked in kirsch and were separated by layers of whipped cream. Shan's chocolate mousse was also excellent. Everyone in our little room was given a complimentary after-dinner drink. Dinner for two with wine was $56.

Although the Milton Inn does not have overnight accommodations, there is an interesting place nearby, the Hunt Valley Inn. This is a resort-type place, with a wide variety of activities from tennis to horseback riding. Prices are moderate.

MRS. K'S TOLL HOUSE
SILVER SPRING, MD.

We tried to imagine what the road must have looked like in 1929 — surrounded by the rolling forests and fields of rural Montgomery county and dotted with farms and small towns. And we imagined what it must have been like to stop at a small roadside cottage and pay a toll in order to continue our journey to Colesville.

Today, that small rural road is six lanes wide in spots, and the scenery along it is that of the city, although a certain rural character is retained by the older homes that line the road. The toll house, with its shingled roof and ivy-covered stucco walls, still stands, but the money it collects now buys a country-style meal instead of a ride in the country. The toll house is more than a hundred years old, although no one seems to know exactly how much more. It collected tolls up until the beginning of World War I, was a tavern until prohibition, and then closed until Mrs. Blanche Kreasburg purchased it in 1929 and established Mrs. K's Toll House.

The food is plain fare built around steaks, fried chicken, roast duck, lamb, and broiled fish. All of the dishes are delicious, and the prix fixe meals are reasonably priced—running from $6 to $8.95 for the complete dinner.

ADDRESS: Colesville Road, Silver Spring, Maryland 20910.
Take the Beltway (I-495) Exit 23, go two miles south on Route 29
TELEPHONE: 301-589-3500
FACILITIES: Dining only; Tuesday through Saturday noon
to 2:30 p.m. and 5 to 8:30 p.m., Sunday noon to 8:30 p.m.
Closed Mondays, Christmas Day, and the last two weeks of
August
RESERVATIONS: Required
DRESS: Nice casual to informal
CREDIT CARDS: American Express

We were seated in the window-walled room overlooking the carefully cultivated rose garden. An enormous wooden music box transformed the holes in a round
tin sheet into the strains of waltzes and the popular
music of a hundred years ago. The imposing music box
is only one of hundreds of antiques in the rambling
house. In one of the dining rooms, fifty-six early American pressed glass plates, with famous designs like Nail-
head, Daisy, Maltese Cross, form an unusual window
decoration. In another room there is a collection of English Staffordshire "Old Blue" pottery made from 1780
to 1830.

At Christmas time, the inn is famed for its display
of Christmas decorations, both modern and antique. The
displays are so popular that reservations for Christmas
season meals are usually booked up months in advance.

We enjoyed the relish dish and the excellent gaz-
pacho, and the towering portions of the main dishes. We
arrived with friends and all ordered different dishes,
so by the time the meal had ended we had a taste of just
about everything on the menu. Every item is recommended.

It's the small touches that set inns apart from
restaurants. We found the small dish of lemon sherbet
served with the main course to be a unique touch—it
was served to cleanse the palate between courses.

After dining we strolled through the house looking
at the antiques. One product of a whimsical inventor was
my favorite: the hickory, dickory clock. This was a clock
about four feet high and shaped like a grandfather's
clock. But in place of the clock face and weights, there
was a wooden mouse that followed a track up past the
rules marking each hour; when the mouse reached one,
it started back down again.

NORMANDY FARMS INN
POTOMAC, MD.

At the turn of the century this was a country barn made of a rigid frame of huge trees hewn into the shape of beams. Today, it is a country inn, with the distinct flavor of Normandy. The beams have been smoothed and polished and painted with the scores and words to traditional French songs. A fabulous collection of copper cookware hung on two gargantuan fireplaces dominates each end of the long pitch-roofed hall.

The dark wooden beams, white plaster walls, French provincial furniture, and collection of lanterns and lights blend with the candlelight from each table to produce an atmosphere that is relaxed and informal. The words to *On The Bridge of Avignon* were inscribed on the log header that formed part of the ceiling wall next to the front fireplace.

We started our meal with a tasty French onion soup. The salad that followed was a bit bland, covered with what tasted like a commercially bought dressing.

I ordered Alaskan king crab *au gratin,* and what I received was good and well prepared, full of huge chunks of crabmeat. Although you may also order the lump crabmeat *au gratin,* it is much better sautéed. The bed of rice on which the *au gratin* version was served was

ADDRESS: Falls Road (Route 189), Potomac, Maryland 20854
TELEPHONE: 301-652-9421
FACILITIES: Dining only; daily from noon to midnight.
Closed Christmas Eve
RESERVATIONS: Recommended weekdays, not accepted on
weekends
DRESS: Informal
CREDIT CARDS: American Express, BankAmericard, Carte
Blanche, Diner's Club

overcooked and had been allowed to dry out.

Shan ordered beef stroganoff and received a rather
bland mixture of sauce and a few chunks of meat over
a bed of wild rice.

Besides the atmosphere, the highlight of the meal
was the arrival of the huge, flaky popovers hot from the
oven. I could have made a meal off them alone. Shan,
being an inveterate tea drinker, was impressed with the
large size of the teapot she received. "Why should coffee
drinkers get all they want while tea drinkers are usually
stuck with a cup or a cup-and-a-half?" she said in remark-
ing on the convenience of the pot that held more than
two cups.

For dessert, I ordered lemon chiffon cake and Shan
ordered cheese cake. The lemon chiffon cake and a lemon
cream cake are the only desserts that the inn makes in its
own kitchens. All other pies and cakes are bought, which
explains why the lemon chiffon pie was very good while
the cheese cake tasted as if it could have come from the
A & P. A meal for two cost about $27.

OLD ANGLER'S INN
POTOMAC, MD.

The Old Angler's Inn sits just across the road from the C&O Canal about fifteen minutes from the Nation's Capital, amid an area rich in history and recreational opportunities. There are indeed some old anglers frequenting the fishing waters here, but the more usual visitor to the area is a cycler or hiker anxious to try out the canal towpath or a history buff visiting the canal's locks and the nearby restored Great Falls Tavern.

The inn was built in 1860 and served many travelers, including couriers and spies from both the Union and the Confederacy. Teddy Roosevelt visited the area frequently in pursuit of the outdoor activities for which he is so well known.

The inn has earned a rather deserved reputation in recent years for not being the friendliest of places. We just did not feel our presence was welcome or our patronage appreciated. Apparently, others have had the same experience. During his march to save the C&O Canal from being made into a super highway (an act that would have caused the inn to be demolished), Supreme Court Justice William O. Douglas and a group of fellow hikers sought refuge at the inn from a thunderstorm and were unceremoniously turned away for being unsuitably attired.

ADDRESS: 10801 McArthur Boulevard, Potomac, Maryland 20854. Take the Beltway (I-495) toward Carderock and Great Falls; follow the road until it ends at McArthur Blvd. Turn left; the inn will be on your right about two miles further
TELEPHONE: 301-365-2425
FACILITIES: Dining only; in winter open Tuesday through Friday from 5 p.m. to midnight, Saturday and Sunday noon to midnight. In summer, Tuesday through Sunday from noon to midnight
RESERVATIONS: Recommended Friday through Sunday
DRESS: Nice casual to informal
CREDIT CARDS: American Express, Carte Blanche, Diner's Club

The English basement-like first floor taproom is a comfortable room filled with overstuffed furniture, ideal for relaxing with a group of close friends by the fire on a cold winter evening. The coziness and warmth of this setting offsets the impersonal demeanor of the staff, and is the only setting in which we would recommend the inn.

The upstairs dining room is decorated with murals of C&O Canal scenes and fishing nets. We arrived somewhat early in the evening, 7 p.m., and after ordering were told that the kitchen was out of the lamb we wanted. The service was slow, and twenty minutes after ordering I received the crock of onion soup I ordered. It was bland, with soggy bread filling most of its volume. The Caesar salad was nicely prepared with not too much dressing but was sprinkled with the uniform, machine-made croutons one pours from a box. I ordered crab imperial, touted on the menu as a restaurant specialty, and Shan ordered the Cornish hen. The crab imperial was adequate as was the hen, though neither was anything to rave about. The vegetable that accompanied both dishes—French-cut green beans— was unseasoned and appeared to have just been thawed out and heated up. We left before trying dessert. Dinner for two was about $30.

The tables upstairs are close together, and even though there were only three other tables of people in the dining room, we were all seated right next to each other.

Apparently, the Old Anglers Inn used to be much better; we had heard so many favorable comments from friends before going. However, our future visits will be confined to the taproom and only if we happen to be nearby; it's not worth making a special trip for.

OLD SOUTH MOUNTAIN INN
BOONSBORO, MD.

As the nation moved west across the Appalachians, families in wagons pulled by oxen and solitary riders on horseback made their way along the National Road (long before it became known as that). They moved slowly by today's standards, and were without even the most rudimentary luxuries except for those rare times when they would arrive at an inn. Then, those that could afford to would buy a meal, a bath, or a place to sleep for the night.

Turner's Gap on South Mountain in Maryland was a major stopping place between the eastern mountains. The Old South Mountain Inn was founded here about 1732 and was a favorite with the pioneers; it was later made a stagecoach stop after the National Road was paved in 1820. The father of the National Road, Henry Clay, stopped here often, as did Daniel Webster and other Washington leaders of that time. The Old South Mountain Inn still caters to thirsty and hungry travelers, although they are more likely to arrive in air-conditioned cars on the smooth two-lane highway than in Conestoga wagons.

The inn continued to play a role in the events of the developing nation as the Civil War got underway. In 1859 John Brown and his raiding party seized the inn

ADDRESS: Alternate Route 40, about three miles east of
Boonsboro, Maryland 21713
TELEPHONE: 301-432-6155
FACILITIES: Dining only; Tuesday through Sunday from
noon until 9 p.m.
RESERVATIONS: Recommended
DRESS: Nice casual to informal
CREDIT CARDS: American Express

and used it as a staging point for their raid on the federal armory at nearby Harper's Ferry.

Three years later, Confederate General D. H. Hill used the inn as his headquarters in a preliminary battle leading up to the gruesome one that was fought at Antietam. The Antietam Battlefield, which is a national park, is located nearby. You can take a guided tour through the countryside that was the sight of one of the bloodiest battles in all of military history. The exhibits that are located in the visitor's center do an incredibly moving job of portraying the suffering and agony of Antietam and of the entire Civil War. If you never visit another Civil War battlefield, visit this one.

The Old South Mountain Inn became a private residence in the late 1800's after the business along the National Road declined due to the growth of the railroads. The preservation of the building is largely attributed to former owner Mrs. Madeline Dahlgren, who also built a chapel in honor of her late husband. The chapel, behind the inn, is now open to the public.

The building became a tavern again in the mid 1920's and served as a local watering hole until it was bought in 1971 by Charles and Dorothea Reichmuth, who restored the interior.

The inn has three main areas—a tavern, a larger dining room, and an outside dining area on a patio that is shaded by a massive wisteria arbor.

The meal includes an enormous relish and fresh vegetable tray that could be a meal in itself. In addition to the typical country fare—ham, chicken, and steaks—the chef does an admirable job on dishes like chicken kiev, veal scallopine, and on a wide variety of seafood dishes. The soups are all homemade and delicious. Dinner for two cost $17.

OLNEY INN
OLNEY, MD.

John Singleton Mosby —
Colonel J. S. Mosby, The
Grey Ghost — terrorized
Northern Virginia and
central Maryland during the Civil War with his lightning
guerrilla raids and daring escapades. He robbed Union
banks, stole its horses, kidnapped its generals, and was
one of the first to embarrass General Custer long before
either man had heard of the Little Bighorn.

It was just after a daring bank robbery held to finance the Confederate cause that the Colonel and his
merry band of marauders, whom some likened to Robin
Hood and his men, came galloping through Olney, Maryland, with the Federals hot on their tracks. In a grove
of oak trees, about two hundred yards from the road,
they spotted a mansion and made straight for it. The
owner was a Southern sympathizer, who hid the cunning
Confederate and his men at great risk to himself.

Well, Mosby got away, and after the war became a
well-respected lawyer in the District. The mansion where
he hid is now the Olney Inn. Built about 1835 the inn has
been a favorite place with area residents and with Presidents. Franklin D. Roosevelt came to the inn so frequently
during World War II that ramps were installed for his
wheelchair long before most public facilities were so
equipped. The ramps still remain. The present maître d',

ADDRESS: Route 108, Olney, Maryland 20832. Take Route 97, Georgia Avenue, and turn right on Route 108
TELEPHONE: 301-924-2121
FACILITIES: Dining, theater; food served Monday through Saturday from noon to 3 p.m. and from 5:30 to 9 p.m., Sundays from noon to 9 p.m.
RESERVATIONS: Recommended a day or two in advance
DRESS: Nice casual to informal
CREDIT CARDS: American Express, BankAmericard, Master Charge

Cliff Robinson, waited on FDR many times and, at the age of 73, is still going strong.

Harry Simms, the inn's owner, is a gregarious person who likes to see his diners satisfied.

Although a variety of items are available from a small à la carte menu, the fixed price dinners are the real bargains. Dishes like roast lamb with mint jelly, country ham, fresh broiled fish, and the inn's specialty, smothered chicken, would satisfy even a Confederate raider, hungry after a day of robbing banks. The entrées are accompanied by homemade breads and rum buns, a beverage, and a deep dish fruit cobbler à la mode. The prix fixe for the entire meal is $7.95.

The Olney Theatre is right next door, and special dinner and theater combinations are available, allowing savings on both the meal and the entertainment. The theater usually offers five plays a summer, with each play running about three weeks. Plays have been performed here since 1942, when it began as an extension of the Catholic University Theater. Olney Theatre seats 720 people, which makes it one of the largest summer theaters. Performances are given every night except Monday. There is a matinée on Sundays.

An antique shop is also located in the converted barn with the inn and the theater.

PETER PAN INN
FREDERICK, MD.

As we passed by the farms and fields of the Maryland countryside, it was hard to believe that just minutes before we had left the frantic pace of Interstate 270. After going through the tiny town of Urbana and bearing right at the fork onto Route 355, a white wrought-iron decorated palace with fountains spouting water appeared on our left. A hundred yards further on, we found the white brick pillar entrance and turned in. The first sight that greeted us was a peacock cage with a pea hen and a cock sitting on top of their fenced-in shelter.

The Peter Pan Inn was started in 1926 by Mrs. Grace Baumgardner, who took what was then a 77-year-old farm house and started a small roadside café. The house, which is now located in the center of a half dozen additions that have been added in the past fifty years, was built in 1849. Mrs. Baumgardner's enterprise was so successful that she added new rooms topsy-turvy. Today, the inn is a mélange of architectural styles that range from French rococo to American, Victorian, art nouveau, and a touch of the neo-classic. The final result is a place that can seat an incredibly large number of people in a variety of rooms that sharply differ in atmosphere.

ADDRESS: Urbana, Maryland 21701. Take I-270 to Route 80 Exit; go through Urbana and turn right at Route 355. The inn will be on your left
TELEPHONE: 301-874-2222
FACILITIES: Dining only; open June 15 to Labor Day daily from noon to 9 p.m.; rest of year Monday through Friday from 4 to 9 p.m., Saturdays and Sundays (and holidays) from noon to 9 p.m. Closed Christmas Day
RESERVATIONS: Not taken
DRESS: Nice casual to informal
CREDIT CARDS: None

The method of ordering meals is also unconventional. Upon arriving, we were greeted by what looks like a carryout window with a menu painted on the wall. We ordered our prix fixe meal here, paid for it, and took the check into the dining room. If you want something to drink, you order and pay for it at your table. Our smiling waitress arrived with a relish tray covered with home-made chow chow, apple butter, cole slaw, and cottage cheese. She took our checks and returned with a basket filled with bran and corn muffins hot enough to melt cold butter. Then came the entrées—country ham and fried shrimp (fried chicken and steak are also available). The vegetables that accompanied them were a meal in them-selves—corn fritters, sautéed potatoes, pickled beets, and green peas in a mushroom sauce. The limited dessert selection—all ice cream—was the only disappointment, but for a complete meal for two that cost $11.48 plus tip, we couldn't complain.

Why an inn should be named after Peter Pan was a question we put to our hostess after the meal, and we received the following reply. Mrs. Baumgardner was a plate collector and her favorite was one with a scene of what she thought was Peter Pan on it. It turned out that after she named the inn, the figure on the plate was identified as Robin Hood instead. No matter, the name stuck, and portions of the plate collection decorate many of the inn's walls.

The Peter Pan Inn does not take reservations, which can present a problem, especially for Sunday dinners. We were told that on Mother's Day this year, they served nearly 4,000 people all day Sunday.

"Sometimes the wait is as long as four hours," our hostess said, "but the people still wait. They pay for their meals and get their numbered checks, and then some sit outside and play cards until their numbers are called over the loudspeaker; others sometimes take a drive around the countryside.''

The waits may be long, but most people who have eaten there say that it was worth it. We had no wait at all the Saturday we arrived for lunch, since we got there shortly before opening. Unless you like waiting, Sunday dinner should be eaten elsewhere.

Peter Pan offers special rates for children, so the inn is always packed with entire families.

STRAWBERRY INN
NEW MARKET, MD.

The closest thing to heaven on earth is to enjoy your work so much that it seems like play. The second closest thing is to be the guest of such a person.

Ed Rossig was an electrical engineer and held the top engineering management spots for several of the biggest electronic firms in the country. But when the corporate rat race started to look like a maze without an exit, he made his own escape and he moved to the sleepy antiques haven of New Market, Maryland, to open an inn.

We parked our car in front of the Strawberry Inn on New Market's Main Street and crossed the porch, past planter boxes full of strawberry plants. We rang the doorbell, but there was no answer. Finally, after ringing four times, we walked around the corner of the house, through Strawberry Alley, and spotted a man building a log cabin in a lot behind the inn.

"Pardon me," I said. "Do you know anything about the Strawberry Inn?"

He set down the hammer and chisel, wiped his forehead with his handkerchief, and said, "What would you like to know?" He was Ed Rossig.

Today, Ed and his wife, Jane, have two guest rooms

ADDRESS: 17 Main Street, New Market, Maryland 21774. New Market is on Route 144, just off I-70 about 10 miles east of Frederick
TELEPHONE: 301-865-3318
FACILITIES: 2 rooms; open year round. The front door is kept locked; guests receive a key
RATES: $12 for double room with private bath
RESERVATIONS: Recommended
DRESS: Casual
CREDIT CARDS: None

in the century-old house they bought, and they plan three more. All of the work is being done by Ed and Jane, in addition to framing pictures, building the log cabin (which will house his picture framing business), running their Hickory Farms franchise in nearby Frederick, keeping an eye on the antique shop next door (of which they own a part), and restoring other old houses in the Frederick area.

Jane has assumed full managerial responsibility for the Hickory Farms business. Although she enjoys getting out and managing the store, she looks forward to the day when she can operate the inn full time.

We sat on the porch benches and read until the sun dipped below the trees. Then Ed invited us into the living room, where we sat and talked with the other room's guests. Talk eventually got around to the picture framing business, which was then located in the house; so we all went upstairs for a lesson in how to mat and frame pictures. Jane arrived home from work between 9 and 10 p.m. and invited us back down to the living room for some iced tea and cheese.

As I helped fix the iced tea, I realized why this inn was the most special one we visited. Jane and Ed treat the people who stay in their inn as house guests not lodgers, as old friends who stopped by for a night.

We retired about midnight—the house guests to their rooms and the Rossigs to their section of the inn. The Rossigs have done a remarkable job of decorating the rooms. Antique furnishings or reproductions are complemented by the wide-planked floors.

Ed is now in the process of restoring the dining room, and soon hopes to serve one meal per day— breakfast—when it is finished. Right now, guests can eat lunch and dinner at Mealy's Hotel, just down the street.

INDEX

COUNTRY INNS OF MARYLAND, VIRGINIA, AND WEST VIRGINIA

"There is nothing which has yet been contrived by man by which so much happiness is produced as by a good tavern or inn."

—SAMUEL JOHNSON

"Die I must, but let me die drinking in an inn."
—WALTER DE MAP

"Shall I not take mine ease in mine inn?"
—WILLIAM SHAKESPEARE

"A book's an Inn whose patrons' praise depends on seasons and on days, on dispositions, and—in time—not wholly on the landlord's wine."

—RICHARD R. KIRK

"Whoe'er has travell'd life's dull round, where'er his stages may have been, may sigh to think he still has found the warmest welcome at an inn."

—WILLIAM SHENSTONE

"Now spurs the lated traveller apace to gain the timely inn."

—WILLIAM SHAKESPEARE

 WASHINGTONIAN BOOKS